ALEXANDRE KOJÈVE AND THE OUTCOME OF MODERN THOUGHT

F. Roger Devlin

D1447189

University Press of America,® Inc.
Lanham · Boulder · New York · Toronto · Oxford

Copyright © 2004 by
University Press of America,® Inc.
4501 Forbes Boulevard
Suite 200
Lanham, Maryland 20706
UPA Acquisitions Department (301) 459-3366

PO Box 317
Oxford
OX2 9RU, UK

All rights reserved
Printed in the United States of America
British Library Cataloging in Publication Information Available

Library of Congress Control Number: 2004109754
ISBN 0-7618-2959-8 (paperback : alk. ppr.)

To my Mother

TABLE OF CONTENTS

PREFACE   ix

ABBREVIATIONS   xvii

I. AN ANCIENT PROBLEM   1
A. The Discovery of Nature   1
B. Senses of 'Nature' and their Common Core Meaning   2
C. Nature and Essence   3
D. The Problem: Is the Essence of Man Natural?   5
E. Why the Ancients Sought to Answer Affirmatively   7
F. How Classical Philosophy Went About Answering   8
G. How Classical Philosophy Overcame Objections   11

II. THE MODERN PROJECT   15
A. A Revolt from the Classical Teaching   15
B. Hobbes's Rejection of Natural Human Teleology   16
C. Hobbes's Own Understanding of Humanity   19
D. The Natural Source of Hobbesian Humanity   21
E. From the Natural Source to the Nonnatural Essence of Humanity   24
F. From Humanity to Commonwealth   25
G. Some Consequences of Hobbes's Rejection of Classical
      Rationalism   29
H. Difficulties with Hobbes's Teaching   33
I. A Thought Experiment to Bring Out the Ambiguities
      in Hobbes's Teaching   36

J. How Classical Philosophy Could Resolve Hobbes's Difficulties   37
K. How Modern Philosophy Might Resolve the Difficulties without
    Departing from Hobbes's Own Principles   39
L. Carrying the Modern Project Forward   42

III. THE FOUNDATIONS OF A HISTORICIST
    ANTHROPOLOGY   45
A. Kojève's Modern Understanding of Nature   45
B. The Source of Kojèvian Humanity   48
C. Kojève and Hobbes vs. the Classical Teaching   51
D. Kojève vs. Hobbes   55
E. A Philosophy of Freedom   59
F. Freedom and Truth   62
G. Atheism and Mortality   65
H. From the Anthropological Source to the Actual
    Beginning of Humanity   68
I. The Impasse of Mastery   71
J. The Advantage of Slavery   73
K. How Mastery and Slavery Account for Human
    Motivation   76
L. The Origin of Discourse   80
M. A Hegelian Idea of the 'End of Man'   85

IV. THE PHILOSOPHY OF HISTORY   87
A. From Anthropology to History   87
B. The Question of Historiographical Accuracy   90
C. The Historical Realization of Mastery: the Greek *Polis*   92
D. Its Difficulties   94
E. How Classical Philosophy Would Resolve Them   96
F. Self-Destruction of the Master's World   97
G. The Triumph of the Slave: the Roman Empire   99
H. The Historical Significance of Christianity   101
I. The Historical Significance of Speech   104
J. From Feudalism to French Absolutism   106
K. The Enlightenment as a Social Movement   108
L. The Thought of the Age of Enlightenment   111
M. The French Revolution   114

V. THE END OF HISTORY   119
A. The Last New World   119
B. The Union of Real and Ideal   120

C. The Universal Homogeneous State   124
D. A Hegelian World-Revolution   131
E. Philosophy and Tyranny   137
F. From Revolution to Resignation   141
G. Conclusion: the Idea of Historicist Wisdom   146

EPILOGUE   153

BIBLIOGRAPHY   157

PREFACE

The present study aims to set forth the teaching of the twentieth-century Hegelian philosopher Alexandre Kojève. It does so in a manner some readers may find surprising, however: the first two of my five chapters do not deal with Kojève himself. The first chapter is concerned with classical philosophy, by which I mean principally Socrates, Plato and Aristotle. The second chapter is devoted to Thomas Hobbes. I have chosen to approach Kojève in this roundabout way because I am convinced it will be helpful to many readers, including some who may at first be made impatient by it.

The classical doctrine sketched in the first chapter is drawn mostly from the *Republic* of Plato and the ethical and political treatises of Aristotle. It is the basis of two-thousand years of Western thought about man and society, and few readers will find a brief recapitulation useless. Hobbes, in chapter two, is chosen as the best representative of the modern, principally seventeenth-century revolt from the tradition of classical and medieval philosophy. Kojève's Hegelianism I present as the culmination of that revolt: as the outcome, in fact, of modern thought itself.

Indeed, it was a temptation to expand the discussion of prehegelian thought farther. Undoubtedly the historical aspect of the present study would have been enriched by some account of Locke and Rousseau as intermediaries between Hobbes and Hegel. The treatment of the classical doctrine might have been extended to include the differences as well as the similarities between Aristotle and Plato, or between various Platonic dialogues, or the interpretation and adaptation of

Aristotle during the middle ages.   But I believe my study gains in clarity by the severity of the restrictions I have imposed on its historical dimension.   Once the student has a firm grasp of the two anthropological traditions, a grasp most easily acquired close to their sources, it becomes as much a pleasure as a task to follow their various developments.

This book may be considered analogous to a three-voice fugue. Certain philosophical themes from classical antiquity are presented in a simple form in the first chapter.   In the second, Hobbes's early modern account of the same subject matter enters as a kind of counterpoint.   In the third and central chapter, Kojève's late modern 'voice' enters as counterpoint to both, and is clarified by comparison and contrast with each: We are then in a position to examine Kojève's Hegelian philosophy of history and his notorious idea of the 'end of history' in chapters four and five.

Kojève is still not a widely-known figure in the English-speaking world, and some readers may find as brief biographical sketch helpful.

Aleksandr Vladimirovich Kozhevnikov was born in Moscow in 1902 into a wealthy bourgeois family.   His most notable relation was his uncle, the painter Vassili Kandinski; in later years, Kojève corresponded with him on aesthetics and wrote an essay on his work.

After the Bolshevik seizure of power, Kojève was arrested by the Secret Police for trading on the black market, but the family was able to obtain his release.   He was denied admission to the University of Moscow because of his "class origin," and fled across the Polish border about the beginning of 1920.   He succeeded in getting some family jewels smuggled out of Russia, which provided the capital for his travel and study over the next decade.   For six years he studied philosophy and oriental languages in Berlin and Heidelberg.   Among his interests at this time were Buddhism and the phenomenology of Husserl and Heidegger.   He received his doctorate from Heidelberg in 1926 for a thesis on *The Religious Philosophy of Vladimir Soloviev*, written under the direction of Karl Jaspers.

He moved to Paris where, in 1927, he married Cécile Shoutak. The couple had no children; they were divorced in 1931.   It was through her that he met the historian and philosopher of the natural sciences Alexandre Koyré, who had been her brother-in-law from a previous marriage.

From 1928 to 1931 Kojève studied mathematics and physics at the Sorbonne.   Ruined financially in the stock market crash, he supported himself by writing book reviews for Koyré's journal *Recherches philosophiques*. He also wrote but did not publish a fragmentary essay on *Atheism* and a study on *The Idea of Determinism in Classical and Modern Physics*. It was at about this time that Kojève formed a friendship with Leo Strauss. Both participated in a seminar given by Koyré at the École des Hautes-Etudes on "The Religious Philosophy of Hegel." Afterwards, Strauss left for Britain to write a book on Hobbes and Koyré was called to the University of Cairo. Koyré proposed Kojève as his replacement, and for the next five and a half years Kojève devoted the seminar to a line-by-line reading of the *Phenomenology of Spirit*. His audience included Raymond Aron, Maurice Merleau-Ponty, Raymond Queneau, André Breton, Georges Bataille, Gaston Fessard and other well-known figures. At one point, he intended to undertake with Strauss a detailed study of the relation between Hegel and Hobbes, but the project was never carried out.

In the early thirties Kojève met Nina Ivanoff, a young Russian emigrée and student of chemistry; they settled in Vanves, outside Paris, in 1932. Kojève became a French citizen in 1937. When the war broke out, he fled to the south, was active in the resistance, and found time to write a six-hundred page *Outline of a Phenomenology of Right* which he did not bother to publish. At war's end he chose not to return to academic life, instead getting a job in the French Department of Foreign Economic Relations through one of his former students. In 1947 Queneau, with Kojève's permission, collected and published materials from the seminar under the title *Introduction to the Reading of Hegel*. They include lecture transcripts, outlines, textual commentaries in a bilingual, telegraphic style, footnotes added by Kojève at the time of publication, and one previously published article. The book had an enormous, not always acknowledged, influence on French thinkers of the postwar period.

In 1948, Leo Strauss published *On Tyranny*, which used a close reading of Xenophon's dialog *Hiero* as a vehicle for criticizing the principles underlying modern political thought—especially those of twentieth-century political 'science'—in the name of classical philosophy. Kojève, at Strauss's request, reviewed the book. While sharing Strauss's contempt for contemporary positivist-inspired political science, he defended the superiority of modern thought in its Hegelian form to pre-Christian philosophy. Kojève's essay "Tyranny and Wisdom," along with a rejoinder from Strauss, was published in a

second, expanded edition of *On Tyranny* in 1954. It has been described
as the most important philosophical exchange of the twentieth-century.

Kojève rose quickly to a position of influence in the Ministry of
Finance. He was involved in implementation of the Marshall Plan and
served as chief French negotiator for the first General Agreement on
Tariffs and Trade (G.A.T.T.). He assisted in founding the European
Economic Community (now the European Union), and took a keen
interest in what has since become known as the North-South problem
or third world development. He traveled extensively as part of his
work, making his first return trip to Russia in 1957.

On weekends and during periods of illness, Kojève worked on a
series of introductions to a planned 'updating' of the Hegelian system
of science. One of these introductions is a thirteen-hundred page
Attempt at a Reasoned History of Pagan Philosophy from Thales to
Proclus. He also left a two-hundred page fragment on Kant's
speculative philosophy. It is perhaps not surprising that he never got
very far with the updating of Hegel's system which he had thus
introduced. The project seems to have been abandoned in the early
sixties. In 1967 he was persuaded to allow publication of the *History of
Pagan Philosophy*, and saw the first of the three volumes through the
press. He died in June, 1968 while attending a meeting of the E.E.C. in
Brussels. Eight further volumes of his writings, along with numerous
essays, have been published in the years since his death.

One aim of the study which follows is to carry out Kojève's and
Strauss's unrealized project of, in Strauss's words, "a detailed
investigation of the connexion between Hegel and Hobbes." A crucial
difference, however, is that we shall for the most part not work directly
with Hegel himself, but with Kojève's highly personal interpretation of
him. Now, it is not necessary to make a perspicuous distinction
between Kojève and Hegel in order to understand Kojève's writings—
just as, if we were interpreting Plato's *Protagoras*, we would not need
to identify its speeches with the 'true' thought of either Plato or the
historical Protagoras. However, the reader will justifiably wonder what
precisely Kojève's relation to the master is. We shall now try briefly to
satisfy his curiosity.

Kojève seems for the most part to have wanted to discourage
inquiry on this point. He once wrote: "the question of whether Hegel
'really said' what I make him say would seem to be puerile if I have
succeeded in demonstrating all I have to say." Elsewhere, he
characterized his seminar on Hegel as "a work of propaganda designed

to strike the minds [*frapper les esprits*] of his hearers." One critic of Kojève complained that "under the pseudonym of Hegel, [Kojève] exposed a personal way of thinking;" in the margin of his own copy, Kojève added "*bien vu!*" All this merely confirms what careful hearers and readers of Kojève had always thought. Calling his interpretation a mere 'introduction to the reading of Hegel' is like calling the *Summa Theologiae* an introduction to the reading of Aristotle.

The most accurate label I can think of for Kojève is *Hegelian philosopher*. Calling him a philosopher recognizes that he was not primarily—though he was also—a Hegel scholar or commentator. The aim of his writings has more in common with Hegel's own than with conventional academic Hegel studies; his first concern was with philosophical truth itself rather than with what Hegel believed to be true. On the other hand, calling him a Hegelian serves to distinguish him from the sort of writer, frequently an object of his scorn, who is as intent on demonstrating his own 'originality' as in saying anything true or important. Truth is one, errors many; and once someone has attained knowledge, the only way to be original is to be wrong. Kojève came to believe that Hegel had achieved a decisive breakthrough in the philosophical understanding of man—one which, though in need of a certain amount of revision, clarification, and supplementation, was essentially valid for all time to come.

There are two points on which Kojève explicitly distinguishes his position from Hegel's own. First, Kojève charges Hegel with the view that human self-consciousness has a natural or necessary tendency to change and expand to take account of changes in the human world, or (what for a Hegelian amounts to the same thing) that man is naturally a philosopher. Kojève suggests that most men tend to resist any expansion of their consciousness of themselves or of their situation without therefore being less human. The philosopher is a *kind* of human being, one whose activity involves going against his 'natural' stasis. Philosophy is the product of unceasing efforts fully comparable to the 'real' struggles of history. It might be argued that Hegel's words are merely ambiguous, and sometimes can be taken to support Kojève's view.

Much the more important disagreement is Kojève's outright rejection of Hegel's entire philosophy of nature. More is involved in this rejection than the common and probably unfair charges that Hegel sought to replace empirical investigation with armchair theorizing, or that he canonized the science of his own time as 'absolute knowledge.' Modern thought, as we shall see, sharply distinguishes the human realm from the merely natural, whereas for the classical thinkers, humanity was part of a more broadly conceived nature. When Hegel applied his dialectical metaphysics to nonhuman nature, he was, according to Kojève, led into error through the influence of classical monism. However that may be, it is certain that Kojève's dualistic revision of Hegel is in the modern tradition of Hobbes. This is one reason for my claim that it is specifically the Kojèvian version of Hegelianism which should be seen as the fulfillment of the modern project.

Ever since Hegel's own day, there has been disagreement over whether his thought is best understood theistically or atheistically. Kojève, exceptionally for him, goes to some trouble to demonstrate that his interpretation follows the historical Hegel on this point. That argument shall not concern us; suffice it to say that Kojève's own. Hegelianism is thoroughly atheistic. In this, too, his interpretation is squarely in the modern tradition, where Hegel himself may seem to have wavered. (Indeed, this question is closely related to that of *Naturphilosophie*.)

Kojève propounds a theory of 'the desire of desire' as man's specific difference, which he privately admitted was not to be found in Hegel. He saw it as the ultimate source of the struggle for recognition as described by Hegel himself.

There are also clear differences of emphasis between Kojève's interpretation and its original. Hegel relates his famous story of Lord and Bondsman in about ten pages of a five-hundred page book. Kojève, substituting the blunter words Master and Slave, makes this passage the basis for his reading of the entire Hegelian philosophy. This is more than a personal quirk: the said passage relates the emergence of humanity, and is thus of the greatest importance for a consistently modern, dualistic Hegelianism.

In the minds of many, Kojève's name is identified with the extravagant-sounding idea of the "end of history." Some, who know Hegel only by reputation, assume that no great philosopher could have said anything that does not sound perfectly sensible (i.e., to them). They conclude that Kojève must have foisted his own preposterous notions onto the more reputable Hegel. One might simply refer such readers to certain passages from Hegel's own writings, such as *Phenomenology*, paragraphs 594 and 801 (the passage on the 'annulment of time'). It is more important to understand why historicism, of which Hegelian philosophy is the most important example, requires such a notion if it is to remain rationally defensible. I shall argue in Chapter II that some idea of an end of human action is necessary to the coherence even of early, prehistoricist modern thought. In any case, Kojève's uncompromising clarity on this point is a difference of rhetoric or emphasis from Hegel but by no means one of substance.

A final difference between Kojève and Hegel is that of historical situation—even if 'history' in the technical Hegelian sense is past. As Kojève said, "one-hundred-fifty years do not go by for nothing, even if nothing *essentially* new has happened on earth or in heaven." One of Kojève's philosophical motives, for example, was a desire to understand the revolution which had, in his own lifetime, overwhelmed the land of his birth. And his political writings and actions during the postwar period—no less than those of Marx a century before—were an effort to apply, under changed circumstances, the thought of the least 'unworldly' of the great philosophers. When a German publisher brought out a translation of his Hegel lectures, he readily agreed to the title *Hegel: eine Vergegenwärtigung seines Denkens.*

The present study is devoted to Kojève rather than to Hegel directly. I have not, therefore, paused to consider the merits of other Hegel interpretations, nor to assess how true Kojève remained to the letter and intentions of his teacher. I have, however, felt free to supplement my argument with citations directly from Hegel's *Phenomenology* wherever this has appeared useful. I found it so especially when treating the philosophy of history in Chapter IV, where much of Kojève's commentary is in a crabbed, telegraphic style. It is to be understood in such cases that I do not think Kojève intends to depart from Hegel's teaching on the point in question.

I have worked the many page references to Kojève's writings directly into my text (rather than consigning them to endnotes) to aid the reader. *Introduction à la lecture de Hegel* is one of the great philosophical works of the last century, but it is also a confusing jumble. In a letter to Strauss, he called it a book which "as regards its form, is beneath all criticism." One of my aims has been to write the sort of book I wish had been available to guide me through the Kojèvian labyrinth, and the references are designed with that in view.

I would like to thank both Gallimard and Basic Books for permission to translate passages from *Introduction à la lecture de Hegel.* I am also grateful to the University of Chicago Press for permission to quote from the third edition of *On Tyranny* by Leo Strauss. The translations from Kojève's writings included in that volume were prepared by Michael S. Roth and Victor Gourevitch. All other translations from Kojève are my own, except one brief quote on page 68. For the convenience of the English-speaking reader, however, I have added page references to corresponding passages in the English abridged translation *Introduction to the Reading of Hegel*, and to two important translations which have appeared in the journal *Interpretation* (see Bibliography for details). If no English reference follows a quote from *Introduction à la lecture de Hegel*, this means the passage belongs to that sizable part of the work still unavailable in English. The translators of *Outline of a Phenomenology of Right* have made such references unnecessary by including page numbers from the French original in their edition.

Translations from Hegel's *Phänomenologie des Geists* are also my own, made from the sixth edition published by the Felix Meiner Verlag. I have included references by paragraph number to the English translation by A. V. Miller.

F. Roger Devlin
Lexington, VA
April 2004

I. AN ANCIENT PROBLEM

The Greeks, who discovered Nature
philosophically, extended to Man
their "naturalistic" ontology...
-Kojève

A. The Discovery of Nature

The Western tradition owes to presocratic philosophy its first clear formulation of the concept of *physis,* or nature. It was understood by way of contrast with *techne* (art or technique) and *nomos* (convention, custom, or law). Such things as stones, stars, trees, and bears exist by nature, while houses, magistrates, poems, and religious rites exist by art or convention. A fully adequate definition of nature, if one is possible, would provide us with an infallible rule for deciding of anything whether it exists by nature or by art or convention.

There are formidable obstacles to establishing such a definition. In particular, it is rarely or never things, but rather aspects of things, which are conventional or artificial. The magistrate exists by convention qua magistrate, since another man could have been appointed to office instead. But he is a two-eyed-being by nature. Thus the natural and conventional aspects of concrete beings can only be distinguished in thought or speech, that is, abstractly. And the effort of abstraction will often not be as easy as in the case just cited. It would seem obvious, for example, that the magistrate is a man by nature. But on second thought, perhaps only the infant from which the man grew was natural, whereas the man qua (adult) man came to be by a combination of natural growth and conventional education. Disentangling these different aspects is no easy task.

The case of man is in fact the source of all the difficulty. For *techne* and *nomos* are specifically human: animals have no laws, religions, arts, crafts, and so forth. And of course, neither do any other natural beings. Accordingly, whenever something does not exist by nature, or not only by nature, man has been at work. Yet nothing is clearer than that he himself did not originate by art or convention. He begins as a natural being, an animal—and somehow remains one at bottom as long as he lives—even while being the source of all art and convention.

Thus everything comes directly or indirectly from nature. This is not a paradox, nor does it deprive our original distinction of its force. It merely means that art and convention are never creation *ex nihilo*, that these specifically human kinds of production begin with nature (or with previous human productions which themselves ultimately derive from nature).

But the foregoing considerations leave man himself a mystery. How does a natural being produce an artificial world? What is the essential character of the being which does so? The attempt to define nature leads us directly to the necessity of defining man—the question of philosophical anthropology.

B.   Senses of 'Nature' and their Common Core Meaning

So far we have spoken of nature only in the universal sense, as the totality of natural things and aspects of things. But people just as often speak of the nature of particular things or of kinds of things. Trees, for example, are a part of 'nature' in the universal sense, but one may also say that the sprouting of leaves belongs to the nature of trees, or that the sprouting of *these* leaves belongs to the nature of *this* tree. This is not a mere equivocation; the senses are obviously related. In all cases nature is prior to art and convention, and those qualities are called natural which are unaffected by art or convention.

Nature is temporally prior: we see trees being used to make houses but no houses turning into trees. And, although it could not be certainly known to the ancient philosophers, the same temporal priority attaches to universal nature: before the advent of man nothing existed by art or convention.

Furthermore, nature enjoys a kind of 'ontological' priority over artifacts and conventions. Aristotle goes so far as to define priority as nearness to that which is by nature (*Metaphysics*, V, 1018b9-14). Thus,

LIST OF ABBREVIATIONS

CTD	*Le concept, le temps et le discours*
EHRPP	*Essai d'une histoire raisonée de la philosophie paienne*
HMC	"Hegel, Marx and Christianity"
IDPH	"The Idea of Death in the Philosophy of Hegel"
ILH	*Introduction à la lecture de Hegel*
IRH	*Introduction to the Reading of Hegel*
L	*Leviathan*
NE	*Nicomachean Ethics*
OT	*On Tyranny*
PD	*Esquisse d'une phénoménologie du droit*
PG	*Phänomenologie des Geistes*
PPH	*The Political Philosophy of Hobbes*

LIST OF ABBREVIATIONS

CTD	*Le concept, le temps et le discours*
EHRPP	*Essai d'une histoire raisonée de la philosophie paienne*
HMC	"Hegel, Marx and Christianity"
IDPH	"The Idea of Death in the Philosophy of Hegel"
ILH	*Introduction à la lecture de Hegel*
IRH	*Introduction to the Reading of Hegel*
L	*Leviathan*
NE	*Nicomachean Ethics*
OT	*On Tyranny*
PD	*Esquisse d'une phénoménologie du droit*
PG	*Phänomenologie des Geistes*
PPH	*The Political Philosophy of Hobbes*

I. AN ANCIENT PROBLEM

> The Greeks, who discovered Nature
> philosophically, extended to Man
> their "naturalistic" ontology...
> -Kojève

A. The Discovery of Nature

The Western tradition owes to presocratic philosophy its first clear formulation of the concept of *physis,* or nature. It was understood by way of contrast with *techne* (art or technique) and *nomos* (convention, custom, or law). Such things as stones, stars, trees, and bears exist by nature, while houses, magistrates, poems, and religious rites exist by art or convention. A fully adequate definition of nature, if one is possible, would provide us with an infallible rule for deciding of anything whether it exists by nature or by art or convention.

There are formidable obstacles to establishing such a definition. In particular, it is rarely or never things, but rather aspects of things, which are conventional or artificial. The magistrate exists by convention qua magistrate, since another man could have been appointed to office instead. But he is a two-eyed-being by nature. Thus the natural and conventional aspects of concrete beings can only be distinguished in thought or speech, that is, abstractly. And the effort of abstraction will often not be as easy as in the case just cited. It would seem obvious, for example, that the magistrate is a man by nature. But on second thought, perhaps only the infant from which the man grew was natural, whereas the man qua (adult) man came to be by a combination of natural growth and conventional education. Disentangling these different aspects is no easy task.

The case of man is in fact the source of all the difficulty. For *techne* and *nomos* are specifically human: animals have no laws, religions, arts, crafts, and so forth. And of course, neither do any other natural beings. Accordingly, whenever something does not exist by nature, or not only by nature, man has been at work. Yet nothing is clearer than that he himself did not originate by art or convention. He begins as a natural being, an animal—and somehow remains one at bottom as long as he lives—even while being the source of all art and convention.

Thus everything comes directly or indirectly from nature. This is not a paradox, nor does it deprive our original distinction of its force. It merely means that art and convention are never creation *ex nihilo*, that these specifically human kinds of production begin with nature (or with previous human productions which themselves ultimately derive from nature).

But the foregoing considerations leave man himself a mystery. How does a natural being produce an artificial world? What is the essential character of the being which does so? The attempt to define nature leads us directly to the necessity of defining man—the question of philosophical anthropology.

B.   Senses of 'Nature' and their Common Core Meaning

So far we have spoken of nature only in the universal sense, as the totality of natural things and aspects of things. But people just as often speak of the nature of particular things or of kinds of things. Trees, for example, are a part of 'nature' in the universal sense, but one may also say that the sprouting of leaves belongs to the nature of trees, or that the sprouting of *these* leaves belongs to the nature of *this* tree. This is not a mere equivocation; the senses are obviously related. In all cases nature is prior to art and convention, and those qualities are called natural which are unaffected by art or convention.

Nature is temporally prior: we see trees being used to make houses but no houses turning into trees. And, although it could not be certainly known to the ancient philosophers, the same temporal priority attaches to universal nature: before the advent of man nothing existed by art or convention.

Furthermore, nature enjoys a kind of 'ontological' priority over artifacts and conventions. Aristotle goes so far as to define priority as nearness to that which is by nature (*Metaphysics*, V, 1018b9-14). Thus, for example, a particular stone is both hard and the cornerstone of a house, but its hardness is prior to its being a cornerstone, because it is hard by nature and a cornerstone by art. Stones are always and everywhere hard, but they may be here cornerstones, there sculptures, etc. (Similarly with convention: a man is one year a magistrate, another year not; but he requires food at all times, by nature.)

So nature not only comes before art but remains in it and finally survives it. A house has no nature qua house, but—because there is no human creation *ex nihilo*—it has a natural aspect. One could say that stone is the 'nature' of a (stone) house; this sense is not common in later philosophical usage, but is recognized by Aristotle (*Metaphysics*, V, 1014b27-31). In practice, nature in this sense nearly always coincides with matter.[1] Art might be defined as the replacement of natural forms with humanly chosen ones. These forms come to be and pass away, but the natural aspect, the matter, continues to exist. Nature is also opposed to convention as the permanent and universal to the transitory and local: man, for example, fears death by nature, always and everywhere, but he punishes murder one way in Athens, another in Corinth.

In addition to temporal priority and permanence, and doubtless because of them, ancient philosophers often assigned a kind of higher 'dignity' to nature than to art or convention.[2] Commonly it was asserted to be somehow divine, even where material.[3] Nature was considered closer to the sources of all being; those natural philosophers who asserted a prime matter or primary elements seem to have held that only this matter or these elements were 'nature' in the strict sense (see *Metaphysics*, V, 1014b32-35).

---

[1] Strictly speaking, this only applies to artifacts made from 'dead' matter. But landscaping and animal training are human arts. A horse by nature desires food, even while (by human art) performing tricks at the circus—and this desire is 'immaterial.' One might extend the meaning of matter to say that the horse, including its immaterial aspect, is the 'matter' of the trainer's art. But none of this affects our main argument.

[2] Often, but not always. The notion of man's progress by his own efforts was not at all unknown in fifth-century Greece; see Guthrie, *A History of Greek Philosophy*, vol. III, 60-84. But this school of thought lies outside the main classical tradition.

[3] Consider, for example, Aristotle's account of the superlunary world, and the stoics' use of the word 'Zeus' to refer to the visible cosmos.

C. Nature and Essence

We have, then, distinguished three senses of nature, which we may call the universal, specific, and particular, and have developed some of the notions common to all these senses—opposition to human art and convention in virtue of temporal priority, permanence and greater dignity or, possibly, divinity. Now we must look more closely at the specific sense, the sense we have in mind when we speak of the natures of *kinds* of things.

This is often confused with essence. Many people, including some professors of philosophy, would see no difference between saying 'it is in the nature of diamonds to be made of carbon' and 'it is of the essence of diamonds to be made of carbon.' The cause of this confusion is probably the idea of permanence which both terms imply. But each of these statements says something more than 'diamonds are always made of carbon.' 'It is in the nature of diamonds to be made of carbon' means roughly 'diamonds are made of carbon before being affected by human art, and even after being cut and polished their carbon composition remains as a "natural aspect."' 'It is of the essence of diamonds to be made of carbon' means 'if something is not made of carbon it cannot properly be called a diamond, however much it may otherwise have in common with real (carbon) diamonds.' Essences are those aspects or properties of things which correspond to the meanings of our names for them;[4] they are understood in contrast to accidents rather than to art or convention.

The difference between nature and essence becomes evident if we consider not a natural kind like diamonds, but an artificial kind like houses. A house, as we have already said, has no nature qua house; it has merely a natural aspect in the materials of which it is constructed. Its essence, however, is precisely the house qua house, which is not given by nature: the property of 'being suitable for human habitation,' let us say. In Aristotelian terms, the nature of an artifact is its material cause, which is accidental; whereas the essence of an artifact is its formal or final cause, which is given it by man.

In a word, nature determines essence in natural kinds, but the two exclude one another in the products of art and convention. Human art *is* the assigning of nonnatural essences to natural things; man, in effect, says to stones and trees, "You shall no longer be what you have been by nature, but shall become a house instead." 'Natural kind' can be defined

---

[4] Which does not mean that man *determines* essence in bestowing names.

accordingly as 'things which share an essence determined by nature rather than by human action.' 'Nature' in the specific sense is simply the essence of a natural kind.

D.   The Problem: Is the Essence of Man Natural?

Man seems to be a natural kind. He is an animal by the same title as any other. And he has certain natural traits which distinguish his species from all others in the same way as, for example, a Luna moth is distinguished from other moths by its size or wing pattern. But he is distinguished from all else in the world—that is, not merely from other primates or animals or organisms—by being the source of all which is not 'by nature,' of all *techne* and *nomos*.[5] What is it in man which allows him alone to produce an artificial and conventional world?

It is tempting to say we want to define 'human nature,' but we must be careful with that expression. It is clear, first of all, that man has an animal nature as much as does any other species. This includes not only traits which he shares with other animals, but also some unique to his species, *Homo sapiens*. Among the latter are the famous 'opposable thumbs' and the organs of speech. And there is even a doctrine, which we may call 'naturalistic anthropology,' that holds all man's specific differences to be functions of these sorts of physical traits. Speech is a particularly complex form of barking; houses and temples are variations on the hive and nest; the state is a further development of the herd, and so forth—'in the final analysis,' of course. For naturalistic anthropology the problem of accounting for *techne* and *nomos* is an illusion; they are simply names for some of the behavior patterns peculiar to one species of ape.

---

[5]Things may also have their source in chance: for example, misbirths and diseases; these too are 'unnatural'—that is, not part of the nature of any animal species. On the other hand, Aristotle held that they are caused by defects of matter, and matter is obviously part of nature. So he clearly has the specific sense of nature in mind when calling misbirths unnatural. A modern molecular biologist would trace them to some equally natural cause. And diseases can even be traced to the generic natures of microorganisms. Similarly, all 'unnatural,' chance occurrences in the nonhuman world are so only with reference to one natural kind while being caused by natural particulars. By contrast, a house (qua house) is absolutely unnatural—unless it is the effect of a human nature.

But it would be wrong to identify the idea of a 'human nature' with the doctrine of naturalistic anthropology; another understanding of it is possible. One may accept that opposable thumbs, speech organs, and the like are part of the merely animal nature of *Homo sapiens*, but also assert a distinct and permanent *humanity* for which no animal traits provide a sufficient explanation. Man, that is, is distinguished qua animal from other species by his thumbs, but he may also be distinguished qua human being from the rest of the universe by what he makes of his thumbs. The animal *Homo sapiens* is the accidental 'vehicle' for man's humanity. When discussing 'human nature' in what follows, it will be this doctrine rather than naturalistic anthropology that we have in mind.

Plenty of obstacles remain to establishing the content and coherence of such a doctrine. One thing we already know is that it would have to account for the possibility of art and convention, since these are at least important components of what is distinctively human. But we have so far defined nature by way of contrast with art and convention; the terms are mutually exclusive. If we were to define human nature as 'a capacity for art and convention,' we would in effect be asserting a 'nonnature nature.' In other words, 'human nature' would appear to be a contradiction in terms.

Furthermore, *Homo sapiens* clearly forms a natural kind; and even if a *human* being is not equivalent to the ape which serves as his vehicle, each particular human would presumably share in the human nature attached to the species. This means that any human nature would be specific—the same sense in which we speak of the 'nature' of diamonds or spiders.[6] Now, one of the chief marks of a specific nature, of the essence of a natural kind, is *regularity*. A spider of a certain species will regularly spin a web of a certain pattern—will do so, that is, barring external obstacles, genetic defects, or treatment with drugs. But human art shows no such regularity. One thing which distinguishes it from the production of animals is precisely a lack of uniformity, a capacity for

---

[6] This was the most common way of speaking about human nature. It is not the only possible one. Each individual may have a particular nature unalterable by education. This was Schopenhauer's teaching, and is also implied in everyday expressions like 'Peter is good-natured' or 'John has a selfish nature.' And, of course, these two principles can be combined in a single doctrine; just as a regular specific nature of horses does not exclude natural variations in particular horses, a natural essence of humanity can leave room for particular natures. But the majority of philosophers who followed in the tradition of Plato and Aristotle down to the end of the Middle Ages laid much greater stress on the common or specific nature of men.

style and innovation. *Nomos* is similarly diverse. Laws, religious rites and beliefs, mores—these are things that notoriously vary according to time and place; whereas the natural is everywhere the same. Once again, 'human nature' appears to be an oxymoron.

E. Why the Ancients Sought to Answer Affirmatively

The rejection of 'human nature' on these grounds may be justifiable. It may be possible to construct a coherent, systematic, and definitive philosophical anthropology without recourse to the concept. This is what we will call 'the modern project.' The present study will primarily be devoted to one attempt at realizing it. But before examining that attempt, it behooves us to ask why it was not made by any ancient thinker—nor indeed, by any significant thinker before the seventeenth century.[7]

We shall not pause to refute the vulgar prejudice that earlier ages were insufficiently aware of 'cultural diversity;' without such awareness it would have been impossible for them to draw the distinction between nature and convention in the first place.[8] If a universal and unchanging 'human nature' continued to be asserted by philosophers down through the centuries, this was because (1) it was seen as an epistemological necessity, and (2) the concept 'nature' was further developed (principally by Aristotle) so as to make it compatible with observed human diversity.

The motive for insisting on a human nature was that without one, no knowledge of human things was possible. Knowledge (*episteme*) was distinguished by the ancients from opinion (*doxa*) by being valid everywhere and always.[9] Now, knowledge is always *of* something, always has an object: in modern philosophical jargon, it is 'intentional.'

---

[7] This is not to deny that there were thinkers who rejected human nature. But they were generally relativists, rejecting also the possibility of a philosophical anthropology (and most often, of philosophy altogether).

[8] It may be fair to criticize the ancients for 'ethnocentrism' on particular points. Thus it is often said that Aristotle attributed to the perfection of human nature *per se* certain traits which happened to be admired by fourth-century Athenian aristocrats. Be that as it may—the *concept* of human nature could not have arisen in this way. Only the observation of differences between cities or civilizations could prompt the formation of a concept of custom or convention, and of its counterpart, nature.

[9] "The object of knowledge in the strict sense cannot be other than it is" *Posterior Analytics*, I, 70b15-16; "Knowledge is belief about things that are universal and necessary" *NE*, VI, 1140b31.

Knowledge can only be permanent—can only be 'knowledge' in the
proper sense of the term—if its object is permanent. So if we are to have
knowledge of man, he must somehow be permanent. And nature is the
permanent *par excellence*. A horse's need to drink, for example, which
belongs to its natural essence, is permanent in the sense that it is coeval
with the horse and disappears only when the horse dies. On the other
hand, it may satisfy this need at one stream today and another tomorrow;
drinking at a certain stream is an accident, not a part of the animal's
natural essence. According to Aristotle, this means the horse's need to
drink can be known (and thus predicated of horse-generations yet
unborn), whereas the particular manner of the need's satisfaction is
forever relegated to the realm of opinion (and unpredictability).[10] In a
like manner, in all cases where scientific knowledge is possible a natural
essence is present. Thus, if man has no natural essence there can be no
knowledge of human things. Since philosophy does seek such
knowledge, it must posit a natural human essence.

F.   How Classical Philosophy Went About Answering

But the epistemological need for a concept does nothing to prove it
free of contradiction. There have always been those who reject the very
possibility of philosophy, whether regarding human things (positivism)
or regarding anything (nihilism, pyrrhonism). What made the concept
'human nature' not merely necessary but coherent was a further
development of the concept 'nature' itself: what we have come to call the
teleological view of nature.
This was first explicitly formulated in Aristotle's doctrine of final
causes: the oak is (by nature) the final cause of the acorn, just as the
architect's idea is (by art) the final cause of the house. Making ends a
part of what we mean by 'nature' allows us to explain departures from
natural norms. Thus, an acorn might not fulfill its natural end—might not
become an oak, or not a healthy one—due to the imperfections inherent
in its matter or the influence of external forces. Nature is what would
always come about if accidental (internal or external) causes did not
interfere. In the case of some kinds it is even possible that the natural end

---

[10] It will be seen from this example that *episteme* has a more restricted
application than the English 'knowledge;' when we want to be precise we may
render it 'scientific knowledge.' It does not include knowledge of historical,
contingent particulars, nor the practical knowledge the ancients called *techne*,
nor acquaintance—as when one says "I know Peter."

might never actually be fulfilled. This does not contradict the definition of nature as a sort of regularity; it even presupposes it. All members of a species tend toward the same natural end, everywhere and always. But we are concerned only with a regularity 'in principle,' which it might require an effort of abstraction to see. For a *de facto* regularity may be wholly lacking where accidental causes are regularly present. In other words, all members of a natural kind might be more or less botched. And several explanations of why this should especially be so in the case of man are offered, sometimes only implicitly, by Plato and Aristotle, and the tradition of thought deriving from them.

The most fundamental and enduring anthropological doctrine of this classical tradition was expressed by Aristotle in his definition of man as *to zoon logon echon*: the 'rational' or 'speaking' animal. Now, we will entirely mistake this teaching unless we bear in mind that 'reason' is understood here in a different and broader sense than it commonly is today. Indeed, we are so used to the economic understanding of practical rationality and positivist-derived accounts of scientific rationality that one is led to wonder whether 'reason' might not now be a misleading rendering of *logos* as it is used by Plato and Aristotle (or of the schoolmen's *ratio*). *Logos* was, first of all, the capacity for understanding and making statements which permit of being true or false. More specifically, it was what allows us to grasp truths. This stands in contrast, for example, to those modern accounts in which it can only assess the validity of arguments. In the practical domain, reason was held to determine the ends of action (likewise conceived as admitting of truth or error), and not merely to adjust means to arbitrary ends. And it included other aspects less important for our present purposes, such as the ability to perform mathematical operations. There were differences between individual philosophers in this tradition as to the precise purview of reason, of course, and in the middle ages border disputes between reason and faith became a central issue. But the facets we have just enumerated can plausibly be called the core of the classical tradition.

A second classical anthropological tenet was that man, like other animals, has a natural end or *telos* which never changes as long as his species exists.[11] Being the end of a rational animal, it will include a perfect actualization of his rational faculty. From this it is clear that

---

[11] Although this permanent natural end may be *discovered* at some contingent time by a single exemplar of the species, named, for example, 'Aristotle.'

human perfection will little resemble the perfection of the heifer that wins the blue ribbon at the county fair: the good man is not the strong or healthy or handsome one. Indeed, the perfect actualization of reason by itself (that is, considered apart from its animal 'vehicle') would seem to be a kind of wisdom or perfect knowing. And since practical ends are a part of reason's domain, the possessor of wisdom would also be 'wise in his actions,' in other words, morally good.[12]

A third classical anthropological tenet is, in Aristotle's famous formulation, that "man is a political animal." This is more closely related to the definition as a 'rational animal' than we are at first apt to think. For Plato and Aristotle always bore in mind—what many modern thinkers tend to forget—that *logos* is essentially interpersonal. While sensation is proper to particular bodies (whether of *Homo sapiens* or some other animal), the truth or falsity of a statement does not depend on who utters it. Thus, no *human*—that is, rational or speaking—being could grow up isolated from other beings of his kind. Man's natural purpose is found in a kind of association: the *polis* (city, state, or society). It follows that the *polis* exists by nature. The full embodiment of man's humanity would be a fully rational city such as Socrates tried to describe in Plato's *Republic*.

Of course, the anthropology we are outlining will remain fairly empty until we can state in detail what man's natural perfection—'the human good'—is. No single, unambiguous teaching on this point can be distilled from the dialogues of Plato, and some of them, for instance the *Republic* and the *Symposium*, seem to embody very different understandings. Aristotle, on the other hand, does provide us with one thematic discussion of the issue, in the first book of the *Nicomachean Ethics*. His method of investigation is not so different from that of Socrates: he begins by examining commonly held opinions, in this case that the good for man is pleasure, money, or honor; he demonstrates insufficiencies in these unreflective views; and he tries to move from them to a more comprehensive view which preserves their correct but partial insights. For, as he says, all actions aim at some good, and therefore the genuine and highest good is somehow implied in all real actions, including the pursuit of wealth, honor, and pleasure. Aristotle's final doctrine is never reduced to a single formula—unless it be that the human good is *eudaimonia* (happiness, well-being, blessedness), which he admits to be an empty statement by itself—but rather given by the ethical and political treatises as a whole.

---

[12] This is the basis of the Socratic doctrine that wrongdoing is a form of ignorance.

We will not examine the details of that account. One might argue endlessly over particular points; our concern is to bring out the essential features of the classical doctrine, those which provide the principles for the analysis of the particular virtues or forms of government. And clearly one essential principle is that there should *be* a good for the human species. Man's end is really there beneath the contingencies, conventions, and follies of everyday life; it is determined by nature; it existed as soon as the first man was born, shall endure as long as endures the species, and cannot be altered by human act or decision. Every human action, including all we refer to as 'history,' occurs around and about natural well-being, approaching or receding from it, but *it* remains a fixed point.

G.   How Classical Philosophy Overcame Objections

The teleological view of human nature can make room for great diversity of observed behavior while continuing to assert the existence of fixed standards of judgment. The bearing of this on the question of *nomos* should be easy to see. Law (to consider only that sense of *nomos*) varies according to time and place, and is no function of our animal nature. But it does not follow that laws are random or arbitrary. Each body of law is a more or less imperfect attempt to actualize a rational human nature, a nature both constant and essentially distinct from that of any animal (including *Homo sapiens*).

But if we grant the accuracy of this account, we are still compelled to admit that the deviation of rational beings from their natural form or *telos* is far greater than that of merely organic beings from theirs—and this on any possible account of man's nature. It requires a trained eye to pick out and describe the superiority of the blue ribbon heifer over its rivals. But all thoughtful people can see that human societies fall far short of anything one might be tempted to consider a universal ideal standard of rationality or well-being. It seems that a rational nature, if one exists, has greater difficulty actualizing itself than a merely organic one. And it is incumbent upon any upholder of the classical teaching to account for this especially wide gap between natural end and reality in human institutions.

There is no thematic discussion of this issue in the writings of either Plato or Aristotle. Aristotle, indeed, discusses the failure of animals to achieve their natural forms, and attributes it to the imperfections of matter; but it would be implausible to assimilate the imperfections of men and cities to biological deformity. We propose instead three possible types of explanation, each admitting variants which considerations of space prevent us from exploring.

First: there is a permanent conflict between man's rational and animal nature, or as we have phrased it, between the nature of man and of *Homo sapiens*. For, as already stated, the end of animal nature is found in the body while speech is essentially interpersonal or public. Hence, a full realization of rationality in a city would involve the suppression of the private realm, the realm of the body and of the animal nature that informs it. This is the reason for the 'totalitarian' character of the *Republic*: the elimination of modesty, family life, and property.

At the opposite extreme from Socrates' 'just city' stands the behavior of the so-called social insects. The hive, the termite and ant colonies, are sets of behavioral patterns which have evolved through natural selection as effective ways of perpetuating the existence of these natural kinds. In other words, their whole function is exhausted in the preservation and reproduction of the animals' *bodies*; the only 'public interest' is the physical well-being of all the particular animals.[13]

All real human societies involve a compromise between the organic and the rational. All are informed by *logos*, rational speech, whether or not one would want to describe them as 'rational' in a loose commendatory sense. Since reason is in fact only incarnate in a species of animal, it cannot avoid taking account of that animal's needs and desires while trying to actualize its own *telos* in a real society. This tension between the rational and animal goods is as permanent as the nature or natures[14] from which it springs.

Thus it would be a mistake to infer political stability from the fixity of human nature. The conflict between the rational, objective, public side of this nature with the animal, subjective, private side explains a great deal of what we call 'history:' war, revolution, social change, and the like. Although states and societies are in perpetual motion, this motion occurs, so to speak, around certain fixed points; these include their physical setting (planet Earth) and the animal and rational natures of the species which composes them. Since conflicts between the private and public good are determined in part by nature, that is, prior to the contingencies of history, it would be foolish to expect any possible historical event such as the founding of a new regime to put an end to

[13] Naturalistic anthropology, holding that man *is* his animal body, cannot admit the existence of a common good. Hence the apolitical attitude of Epicurus—and Plato's contempt for materialism.

[14] It does not affect our argument whether we speak of one human nature with two aspects or of two natures in one being.

them. Socrates expresses this in the *Republic* by showing how even a fully rational regime could decay into a tyranny. The best we can hope for in practice is a relatively stable regime which compromises with man's animal nature but allows the exercise of the virtues and the pursuit of wisdom. This explains why Plato later found it necessary to write his *Laws* and Aristotle his *Politics*.

Second: in addition to the tension between man qua man and qua *Homo sapiens* there are permanent tensions within the nature of man qua man. We have stated already that *logos* was a broader concept than reason is in most modern thought—in particular, that it includes both the ability to comprehend general truths and the power of speech. Now, it is obvious that we use speech for purposes other than seeking or communicating general truths; for example, there is the pleasure we take in stories or other works of the imagination. And, as Socrates explains in the *Republic*, the aim of reason in seeking truth and the good for man is essentially different from the aim of the imagination in poetry. It follows that the perfect fulfillment of reason's aims will require the suppression of some of imagination's possibilities, and thereby of a part of our humanity.

Poetry, while its aim is not—or not *simply*—truth, could perhaps be assigned to the domain of *logos*, since it is verbal in form. But nonverbal arts such as music fare no better in the philosophical city, and for the same reasons. Yet they too are specific to humanity. And a little reflection calls to mind a host of other things unique to our species yet not simple functions of reason or speech: war, religion, romantic love, games, ceremony, personal sacrifice, work and craftsmanship, friendship and enmity, the sense of personal dignity which the ancients called *thymos*, and many more. Perhaps some or even all of these things could only occur in beings which also possessed the power of speech, but that would have to be demonstrated—and it still would not follow that they are mere *functions* of *logos*. The definition of man as a rational animal should on no account be interpreted to mean that man is nothing but 'animal nature plus reason.'[15]

In the *Republic* Socrates stipulated that all other aspects of human nature—as well as man's animal nature—be wholly subjected to the demands of reason and of reason's embodiment, the perfectly wise ruler.

---

[15] Aristotle recognized this as well: "It seems that passions, which are nonrational, are not less human, and so are those actions which proceed from temper and desire" (presumably meaning specifically human desire) (*NE*, III, 1111b1-2).

In real states, of course, the demands of the various aspects of human nature are arbitrated not by reason alone but by the decisions of fallible rulers, habit, religious and social traditions, and plain compromise. Once again, the tensions are as permanent as the nature from which they arise.

But Aristotle and the Platonic Socrates agreed that reason was *capable* of functioning as a guide to the rest of man's human and animal nature, and that it was generally *desirable* for it to do so (though it would always have to make practical compromises). Both the Humean view of reason as servant to the passions and the romantic glorification of art and sentiment *over* reason are wholly alien to classical philosophy.

Third and most obviously: real societies diverge from the *telos* of rational human nature because of the weakness of human reason itself. In the *Republic* Socrates outlined a program of education for those best suited by nature to the pursuit of wisdom. He asserted that after thirty years of study these philosophers would obtain the vision of the Good, come into possession of the comprehensive truth. From having been philosophers they would become sages. And they would have plenty of time left over to organize their city on a rational basis or to maintain it so organized: they would assume office at an earlier age than most American presidents.

Now, we have excellent reasons for doubting that Plato considered such a scheme realizable. First, Socrates gives no hint as to what steps would be needed to implement it; he merely asserts the possibility of a philosopher by chance becoming king or a king learning to philosophize. Second, there is strong evidence that neither Socrates nor Plato considered *himself* a sage: from Socrates we have the famous statement, "All I know is that I know nothing," from Plato the cultivation of the always more or less 'aporetic' dialogue form in preference to the treatise. Are we to believe either of these men so modest as to think more 'philosophical' natures than their own regularly available in real cities? Third, if Plato considered cities ruled by wisdom a practical possibility, there is no good explanation for his later considering the claims of a 'second best' city. And if this understanding of the relation between the *Republic* and the *Laws* is correct, Plato's and Aristotle's thought would seem to coincide here; for Aristotle also tells us that "one regime is by nature the best everywhere" (*NE*, VI, 1135a5), but clearly recognizes the relative legitimacy of a number of regimes suited to different times and places.

II. THE MODERN PROJECT

Everything you write is correct.
Hegel undoubtedly takes Hobbes
as his point of departure. A
comparison is surely worthwhile...
- Kojève, Letter to Leo Strauss

A. A Revolt from the Classical Teaching

Teleological accounts of man—in pagan or Christianized form, and each admitting indefinite variation—dominated philosophical speculation for around two thousand years. But, as we have already remarked, there is no *logical* necessity about this; we have not yet proved that a coherent nonteleological anthropology is impossible. It is perfectly imaginable that art and convention do not represent any sort of groping toward a dimly sensed, preexisting end. They may be nothing more than alterations of or additions to the natural order whose only 'purpose' is to fulfill the blind desires of the individuals or societies which bring them forth. This would seem to make scientific knowledge of human things impossible; anthropology, the reasoned account of man's timeless nature, would have to give way to a simple listing of the conventions he had in point of fact instituted in various times and places, and of the arts he had acquired. It would also eliminate the standards provided by the ancient philosophers (the just city, the great-souled man) for evaluating the real human world. In a word, it would destroy the basis of classical ethical and political science, apparently without putting anything in its place.

Modern philosophy is in large measure a series of attempts to resolve this difficulty. The sources of this revolution in thought are complex. One was the revolt against teleological explanation in the philosophy of lifeless things, that is, in what we have come to call the science of physics. If natural ends can profitably be banished from physics, why not also from the human sciences? Another source was the political thought of Machiavelli, who rejected the appeal to a single, ideally just human order as both unrealistic and harmful to practice: "there is so great a distance between how one lives and how one ought to live that he who rejects what people do in favor of what one ought to do, brings about his ruin rather than his preservation" (*The Prince*, xv). And a third source was reformed theology, which asserted a more thorough corruption of human reason by sin than the Christian Aristotelians had allowed, holding it wholly unable to discover or pursue man's true end.

B.   Hobbes's Rejection of Natural Human Teleology

But rather than pausing to trace these historical origins we prefer to consider the first fully articulated modern philosophical anthropology: that of Thomas Hobbes.

Now, there is no such thing as a complete revolution in thought, and every new philosophical teaching shares something with its predecessors. Hobbes shared with his whipping boy Aristotle the principle that nature is the proper starting point for thinking about man. And for both, nature is an eternal order which 'somehow' underlies the eternally changing world of human affairs. But for Hobbes nature does not underlie art and convention in such a way as to provide standards for understanding and judging them.

The source of most of the important differences between Hobbes and the tradition of thought he was attacking is his restoration of the presocratic opposition between *physis* and *nomos,* which had been weakened by Plato and Aristotle: the human things were again to be understood in contrast to, rather than as a part of, nature. He made this opposition the very starting point of his speculations:

> Two chief kinds of bodies, and very different from one another, offer themselves to such as search after their generation and properties; one whereof being the work of nature, is called a *natural body*, the other is called a *commonwealth*, and is made by the wills and agreement of men. And from these spring the two parts of philosophy, called *natural* and *civil* (*De Corpore*, I, I, §9).[1]

---

[1] We see from this citation also that Hobbes accepts the classical teaching according to which the state is the comprehensively human reality.

Thus, for Hobbes, nature merely sets the stage for human action, or provides the material on which it works.

Accordingly, Hobbes repeatedly attacked the idea of a natural human *telos*. "There is no such *finis ultimus* (utmost aim) nor *summum bonum* (greatest good) as is spoken of in the books of the old moral philosophers" (*L*, xi). And in another place: "For suppose that the *finis ultimus* has been reached: then nothing more will be desired. It follows that from this point on there is no good for man, indeed, that men feel nothing anymore. For every sensation is linked with a desire or aversion, and not to sense means not to live" (*De Homine*, xi, §15). And again: "Men justly complain as of a great grief, that they know not what to do" (*Elements of Law*, I, vii, §7).

Now, if we take this criticism at face value, we shall have to conclude that it is rather silly. Aristotle clearly defined the human end of *eudaimonia* as a form of activity, not as a cessation from activity.[2] Hobbes's attribution of absurdity to him exploits the ambiguity in the word 'end,' probably deliberately. But, though it lies deeper than his polemic lets appear, the difference between his and the traditional account of human desire and action is both real and of the greatest importance.

According to Aristotle, animals as well as men have a natural end, and theirs also is no state of rest. The end of bears, for example, is to *be* bears, and this means doing what is necessary for the preservation of both individual and species. A bear typically spends its time chasing bear food, sleeping, avoiding threats to its existence, and occasionally mating. For short intervals, when all its desires are satisfied, it may simply lie in the sun. But its life has no *finis ultimus* such as is asserted by Hobbes's imaginary philosophers: the same set of bear desires eventually returns. Characteristic of animals is precisely that it is the *same* set of desires which returns, bringing about the same sorts of behavior. A bear's stomach is full, then empty, then full again; its desire to mate leads to the birth of a cub which grows into a bear with the desire to mate. Thus, while a living bear is never completely at rest, there is a natural permanence underlying all its movements: they are 'cyclical.' All essential animal movements partake of this permanent or cyclical character. There are also, however, accidental aspects of animal movement which cannot be explained: for example, whether

---

[2]Aristotle does speak of "men always [wanting] more and more without end; for it is of the nature of desire to be unlimited" (*Politics*, II, 1267b15). But even here he adds that it is only "most men" who live for the gratification of such desire.

this bear on *this* day catches its third salmon with its right or left forepaw.

Clearly there are aspects of human action which fit the cyclical pattern of animal life and others which are merely accidental. But many characteristically human actions do not fall into either category. The invention of a machine brings something essentially new into the world, since the essence of the machine is different from the natural essence of the materials from which it is constructed. The founding of a state does not repeat an earlier founding: the Holy Roman Empire proclaimed in AD 800 was not the same Roman Empire which had existed from 31 BC to AD 476. Let us describe these sorts of actions as 'linear.' Hobbes's denial of a human *telos* can be understood as an insistence upon the linear as opposed to cyclical pattern of specifically human action. In this respect it may seem clearly superior to classical thought. But before we jump to such a conclusion we must ask whether classical philosophy really provides no way of accounting for the linear aspect of human action.

Indeed, it does have a way of so accounting. We must bear in mind that teleological anthropology does not entail the claim that man's end has ever been actualized, or even that it could be. But if it were, it would in fact give human life a cyclical character. Such, at any rate, appears to be the lesson of the *Republic*. In the ideal city every rational person would be entirely 'conservative' in politics, since any change of institutions would necessarily lack rational justification. Governance would become a kind of maintenance—or at most, of progress along well-defined lines, as in the ongoing eugenics program. In addition to the vital cycles *Homo sapiens* shares with other animals, human life would include 'rational cycles'—such as the unchanging thirty year education in wisdom given to each rising generation of philosophical natures. Since the rulers are assumed to be in possession of Truth, we must imagine that all the possibilities of technology would be open to them. They, in their wisdom, would establish the level and kind which best serve their city. In a word, human life would outwardly come to resemble the self-perpetuating, cyclical lives of animals. The crucial difference would be the self-consciousness of human life. Differently put, the permanence of animal life is grounded in that of their natural *being*; the permanence of fully actualized humanity would be grounded in the eternal character of *truth* (especially the 'true good for man').

According to classical anthropology, man is suspended awkwardly between two sorts of natural perfection. Unable to descend to the cycle of purely animal nature, neither can he fully actualize his rational nature. He is a wanderer without apparent direction. But the philosopher can, albeit imperfectly, extrapolate man's true end from his confused strivings. The cyclical life of the *Republic* can, if Socrates has got it right, serve as a point of repair for comprehending linear movements such as political revolutions. For example, the replacement of an oligarchic by a democratic regime can be understood as a movement away from rational perfection toward a life governed by animal desires. Or again, the establishment of a timocracy is favored by, and favors, *thymos* at the expense of other human possibilities. History, meaningless in itself, is thus given meaning by its timeless natural sources. As for the linear development of the arts, or 'technological progress,' it is at the mercy of (cyclical?) natural cataclysms. Thus Aristotle reconciled human inventiveness and the progress of philosophy from Thales to himself, with the eternity of the world.

C.   Hobbes's Own Understanding of Humanity

There can be no doubt that Hobbes meant to deny the existence of a natural end of man not merely in the ridiculous sense he makes explicit, but also in the sense we have just outlined. According to the Hobbesian anthropology man's actions are not merely linear *per accidens*, that is, because he cannot in fact attain his natural end, but essentially and in principle: there is no such end to be attained. For, first of all, there is no true good for man:

> Whatsoever is the object of any man's appetite or desire, that it is which he for his part calleth good; and the object of his hate and aversion, evil.... For these words of good [and] evil...are ever used with relation to the person that useth them, there being nothing simply and absolutely so, nor any common rule of good and evil to be taken from the nature of the objects themselves (*L*, vi).

In other words, the passions are a more fundamental anthropological fact than their objects. For the self-sufficient rational activity over the course of a whole human life, that is, for what Aristotle called *eudaimonia*, Hobbes substitutes 'felicity,' defined as "*continual success* in obtaining those things [sc., whatever they are] which a man from time to time desireth" (*L*, vi).

Second, human desire is infinite. All desire is for some apparent good (Hobbes agrees with Plato and Aristotle), and "the POWER of a man is his present means to obtain some future apparent good" (*L*, x). And "a perpetual and restless desire for power after power, that ceaseth only in death" is "a general inclination of all mankind" (*L*, xi). Moreover, power is a means not only to apparent goods but to further means to them, that is, to greater power: "for the nature of power is in this point like to fame, increasing as it proceeds" (*L*, x). Similarly, when human (as opposed to animal) desire attains its momentary object it fixes on another, usually greater one. "Men from their very birth and naturally, scramble for everything they covet, and would have all the world, if they could, to fear and obey them" (*Decameron Physiologicum*, in *English Works*, vol. 7, 73). In short, human desire is not endless merely in the sense that it continually returns like animal desire; it is inherently insatiable. Man is 'Faustian.'

Let us, to illustrate, compare the classical and Hobbesian teachings with regard to one important form of power, viz., wealth. Aristotle was as aware as Hobbes that many men desire wealth without limit. But on his view such men confuse means with ends. Wealth, understood properly, is a means to right living. Some knowledge of that end is therefore required before one can give a scientific account of wealth, its acquisition and use. To devote one's life to acquiring the *means* of living is contrary to the natural order, the effect of a vice called *pleonexia*.[3]

Hobbes, by contrast, explains 'covetousness' as: "a name used always in signification of blame, because men contending for [riches] are displeased with one another's attaining them, though the desire in itself be to be blamed or allowed according to the means by which these riches are sought" (*L*, vi). In other words, what Aristotle took to be a vice peculiar to certain people is the natural, universal, and unalterable condition of man; the virtue contrary to *pleonexia* does not exist.

Without any natural limit to human desire it appears that there can no longer be any natural standard by which human institutions and productions might be understood and judged. Instead of a single timeless account of man, we are reduced to mere noting of what man has in fact instituted and produced, coupled with the prospect that the 'line' of his action may veer in another direction tomorrow. Where we thought we had science we now have, at best, historical knowledge; where there had appeared necessity there now appears contingency;

---

[3]*Politics*, I, 1257b26-1258a14.   Hobbes gives the typically modern mistranslation of *pleonexia* as a desire of more *than one's share*: see *L*, xv.

where Aristotle had stood we now meet Heraclitus. And most importantly, we are deprived of the standards of conduct which formerly had been derived from man's supposedly fixed natural end.

Hobbes denied that these are necessary consequences of rejecting the teleological understanding of human nature. He claimed that his understanding of man, that is, the true, nonteleological one, issued in a true account of human institutions both as they are and as they should be. We will now look at how he set about trying to make good this claim, and attempt to determine how far he succeeded.

D. The Natural Source of Hobbesian Humanity

Rejecting Aristotle's doctrine that "the end of a thing is its nature," Hobbes rejected the corresponding view of philosophy as concerned with ends; for him it becomes an understanding of genesis:

By PHILOSOPHY is understood the knowledge acquired by reasoning from the manner of the generation of anything to the properties, or from the properties to some possible way of generation of the same; to the end to be able to produce, as far as matter and human force permit, such effects as human life requireth (L, xlvi; compare definition of science in L, v).

Hobbesian anthropology, then, is first of all a 'reasoning from the properties' of man as he is observed now to an account of how he could have become so. This is the method Hobbes used in formulating his famous and influential doctrine of the 'state of nature.' Secondly, reversing direction, that knowledge of the generation of human properties is applied to "produce...such effects as human life requireth." This is the procedure he used, or claimed to use, to arrive at his recommendations for political practice. We shall follow the same order in our exposition.

For Hobbes no less than for the ancients it is a central problem of philosophy to explain the seemingly paradoxical 'human nature'—that is, the relation between nature and nonnature *in* the one kind of natural being which is at the root of all that is not 'by nature.' But he rejects the classical solution, viz., the notion of a 'higher' nature inadequately expressed in speech and reason, calling forth and informing human productions and institutions. Perhaps the most striking expression of this revolt from classical anthropology is his characterizing speech as an "invention" analogous to printing and writing. As with any invention, speech was originally intended to serve practical purposes. It was, for example, a help to human *laziness*, "registering...the consequences of our thoughts which, being apt to slip out of our memory and put us to a new labor, may again be recalled by such words as they were marked by."[4] The other aspect of the ancient *logos*, viz., reason, presupposes speech, and hence is even farther removed from man's nature.

Having rejected the traditional definition of man, Hobbes must either point to some other natural trait which distinguishes him (and on the basis of which the invention of *logos* can be explained) or accept the thesis of 'naturalistic anthropology:' speech is barking, the state is a hive, etc. Hobbes took the first path. After discussing sense, memory, imagination, understanding, and the "unguided train of thoughts," and remarking in most cases on their presence in both men and beasts, he comes to the "regulated train of thoughts." It "is of two kinds: one, when of an effect imagined we seek the causes or means that produce it; and this is common to man and beast. The other is, when imagining anything whatsoever, we seek all the possible effects that can by it be produced—that is to say, we imagine what we can do with it when we have it—of which I have not at any time seen any sign but in man only."[5]

The fundamental human thought is not 'Where did it come from?' (which is at least quasi-teleological—an account of how an end, albeit not necessarily a natural one, is reached), but 'What can I do with it?' (which 'posits' an end to be reached through knowledge and control of efficient causes).

As to the significance of this innovation for the rest of Hobbes's thought, we cannot improve on the commentary of Leo Strauss:

> The reason why Hobbes transformed the traditional definition of man as the rational animal into the definition of man as the animal which can "inquire consequences" and hence which is capable of science, that is, "knowledge of consequences," is that the traditional definition

---

[4]*L*, iv. Compare the corollary doctrine in chapter v that "reason is not...born with us, nor gotten by experience only...but attained by industry."

[5]*L*, iii. In chapter vi he defines 'curiosity' as a "*desire* to know why and how," and says that such desire "is in no living creature but *man*." This is difficult to reconcile with chapter iii. But then in chapter xi he adds that "anxiety for the future time" is a chief source of curiosity, "because the knowledge of [causes] maketh men the better able to order the present to their best advantage." In other words, a specifically human *fore*thought may motivate men's inquiries into the past.

implies that man is by nature a social animal, and Hobbes must reject this implication (*De cive*, I, 2). As a consequence, the relation between man's natural peculiarity and speech becomes obscure. On the other hand, Hobbes is able to deduce from his definition of man his characteristic doctrine of man: man alone can consider himself as a cause of possible effects, that is, man can be aware of his power; he can be concerned with power; he can desire to possess power; he can seek confirmation of his wish to be powerful by having his power recognized by others, that is, he can be vain or proud; he can be hungry with future hunger, he can anticipate future dangers, he can be haunted by long-range fear (*What is Political Philosophy?*, 176n).

One can easily see how the 'inquiring of consequences' could be at the root of *techne*, and in a more remote way perhaps of *nomos*. But to establish his teaching in place of the traditional one, Hobbes would first have to show how speech is derived from natural human 'inquiring of consequences,' possibly in combination with other causes or circumstances. This he never does; as Strauss says, their relation is "obscure." Furthermore, immediately after calling speech an invention he characterizes it as a prerequisite for political association; without it "there had been amongst men neither commonwealth nor society nor contract nor peace, no more than amongst lions, bears and wolves" (*L*, iv). But the state of man before the institution of commonwealth is the state of nature. Therefore speech is natural after all. Or else Hobbes's state of nature is not the true one, but already incorporates a good deal of *techne*.

It seems we must distinguish two states of nature: one in which man is distinguished from other natural beings only by the ability to inquire consequences, and another immediately preceding the institution of commonwealth. In the interval, somehow, speech is invented. Since Hobbes lists as the first "general use" of speech that "names...serve for *marks* or *notes* of remembrance," it may seem that it was invented by particular men in natural, Crusoe-like isolation from one another. Implausible as this sounds, it would be the only way for him to avoid maintaining the natural priority of some sort of society to speech—and that, in turn, would come very close to maintaining the naturalness of society altogether.

We believe it impossible to determine unambiguously what Hobbes's 'true' teaching about speech is; his statements are brief and contradictory.[6] But we believe Strauss is correct as to the *motive* for his

---

[6]"Invention" could, of course, be interpreted as referring merely to the conventionality of morphemes, that is, that dogs can just as well be called

denial of the naturalness of speech. Hobbes saw as well as Aristotle the intimate relation between speech and association. For Aristotle this had meant that the *zoon logon echon* was necessarily also a *zoon politikon*; Hobbes, from denying the naturalness of the commonwealth, was led to deny the naturalness of speech itself.

E.   From the Natural Source to the Nonnatural Essence of Humanity

There are other indications that the state of nature immediately preceding the institution of commonwealth is already far removed from 'animal nature plus ability to inquire consequences.' Man in this 'late' state of nature has already done enough causal inquiring to arrive at the notion of "spirits invisible;" the fear of them is "in every man his own religion, which hath place in the nature of man before civil society" (*L*, xiv).[7] There is even a kind of unpolitical association: the family. Thus, as an example of the state of nature *in acto*, Hobbes mentions that "the savage people in many places of America" have only "the government of small families, the concord whereof dependeth on natural lust" (*L*, xiii). This certainly helps explain the apparent contradiction of speech being both natural and an invention.

It is difficult to clarify the relation between these 'early' and 'late' states of nature, since they are never explicitly distinguished by Hobbes himself. We would like to know how the characteristics of the late state of nature are derived from those of the early, whether their derivation corresponds to a real historical process, and what is the metaphysical status of man's 'late nature' *vis-à-vis* nature and convention. Let us suppose, for example, that at one time an animal with the faculty of inquiring into the consequences of things actually existed, and that its descendants are the humans of today. There would have to be a story— no longer fully knowable, but partially reconstructible from its beginning and end points—explaining how the later beings arose from the earlier. This story would be a *historical anthropology*. It would explain how a trait like speaking or glorying could be *essential* to man (meaning that a being without any mental faculty for speech or tendency to glorying would not be quite what we mean by 'human')

---

chiens or *Hunde*. But then Hobbes would seem to have left the power of speech itself natural.

   [7]There is for Hobbes no natural distinction between religion and superstition, which *almost* amounts to calling religion the superstition permitted or enjoined by the sovereign.   .

and *universal* (meaning present and effective under all sorts of regimes, in periods of civil war, regardless of the dominant religion, etc.)—and yet not be *natural* (meaning not actual in the individual prior to education or in the race prior to art or convention). On this account a magistrate, for example, would have two eyes as part of his animal nature, an ability to inquire consequences as his human nature, an ambition for honors and power as part of his nonnatural human essence, and a particular public office by convention.

Hobbes never develops his anthropology in this manner. He says of his (late) state of nature: "I believe it was never generally so over all the world" (*L*, xiii). Presumably he would have considered it still less likely that the early state of nature was ever actual. The 'earliness' of the ability to inquire consequences is easiest to interpret as logical rather than temporal priority; it means that the ability is presupposed by the thoughts and passions of man in the late state of nature without presupposing them in turn. And the same may be true of the late state of nature's priority to commonwealth. In sum, the rejection of teleology combined with the inconsistencies in the Hobbesian account of nature were the seeds from which historicism grew—but Hobbes was not a historicist.

F.   From Humanity to Commonwealth

Let this suffice concerning the remote origins of the state of nature. We now want to look at the late, immediately prepolitical version of that state and at the institution of commonwealth that follows upon it. Here Hobbes is a good deal more perspicuous than concerning the first principles of his teaching.

Hobbes shares with the classics the doctrine that the state is the comprehensive expression of humanity. For the classics this meant that the *polis* was the most complete observable actualization of human nature, and a truly complete actualization would be identical with the perfect *polis*. For Hobbes human art and convention transcend, and normally improve upon, nature: "By art is created that great LEVIATHAN called a COMMONWEALTH or STATE" (*L*, Introduction). In the one case the state is the most comprehensively natural (that is, humanly natural) being; in the other case it is the most comprehensively conventional being—that in which all other conventions and all the arts find their place—but thereby likewise the most perfect and most human.

In describing the transition from nature to commonwealth Hobbes is concerned to lay bare the purposes of political association so as to establish objective nonteleological standards for the comprehension and evaluation of political things. He begins by describing a set of passions, that is, of desires, hopes and fears, which he asserts to be common to all men, though he does not assert that their relative strength is identical in all.[8] The *objects* of the passions are not determined by nature: "For these the constitution individual, and particular education...vary" (*L*, Introduction). This means that if there are any universal standards of political conduct they must arise either directly from the passions or from the passions in combination with circumstances or inferences themselves universal—but in no case from the ends men pursue.

Let us suppose that one universal passion leads directly to political association, for example, the fear of death: all men fear death, and this of itself is a sufficient condition for their living in states. Now, this is nothing more than a reassertion of the naturalness of the state. The same would be true of any single passion one could name. If this is how we are to 'derive' the state we might as well ascribe to man a 'political instinct,' and so make the tautology manifest. In other words, if we are serious about the conventionality of the state we cannot derive it directly from a single natural passion. Hobbes's manner of proceeding shows that he was conscious of this.

He names, first of all, three principle passions which tend to dissociate men; these are competition, diffidence and glory. "The first maketh men invade for gain, the second for safety, and the third for reputation." On the other hand, "the passions that incline men to peace are fear of death, desire of such things as are necessary to commodious living, and a hope by their industry to obtain them" (*L*, xiii).

A little reflection will reveal that these two lists overlap considerably. The fear of death may, under the appropriate circumstances, incline us to peace and society, but it is also a reason for diffidence when we are in the state of nature. Desire for the means of commodious living and the hope of attaining them by one's industry motivate the soldier taking part in the sack of a town as well as the thrifty and honest shopkeeper. There is one unambiguous passion, as Hobbes presents it, and it belongs to the antisocial list: glory. While the other passions are educable, that is, can be made useful to man in society, glory nearly always has to be simply suppressed.

---

[8]*De Cive,* I, §4 may seem to indicate the contrary, but it is unclear whether the difference there referred to rests on a difference in the passions or in beliefs.

Glory is at home in the imagination; Hobbes initially defines it as "joy arising from imagination of a man's own power and ability" (*L*, vi). As such it is private, and thus apparently neither social nor antisocial. Trouble arises because "man, whose joy consisteth in comparing himself with other men, can relish nothing but what is eminent" (*L*, xvii). The glorious imaginings of two men necessarily contradict one another: they cannot both be more powerful. They also cannot rest satisfied with their vain imaginings; they must seek objective confirmation of their self-assessment. This is an important supposition of Hobbes's teaching: natural man is not a stoic who can find satisfaction in his own thoughts without regard to the world around him. "As in other things so in men, not the seller but the buyer determines the price. For let a man (as most men do) rate themselves at the highest value they can, yet their true value is no more than it is esteemed by others" (*L*, x).

This has an important implication: man is, on Hobbes's account, a 'social being' in the sense that he has a passion which can only be satisfied by other members of his species; a child suckled by wolves and isolated from other beings of his kind would lack an essentially human quality.[9] Glorying is opposed to society not in the broad sense of 'being independent of human interaction' but in the narrow sense of 'being inimical to peaceful commonwealth.' Hobbes describes with delightful cynicism how men do seek out their fellows—as a means of satisfying their own vanity (*De Cive*, I, §2). The true Hobbesian view was well expressed by Kant in his famous phrase, "man's unsocial sociability."

What happens when a glorying man encounters his fellows in the state of nature? Somehow, by word or deed, he *expresses* his imagination of his own superiority, asserts its objectivity—from which it follows that the others ought properly to recognize it. Strauss again:

> Either the others take his claim seriously and feel themselves slighted, or they do not take his claim seriously and he feels himself slighted. In either case, the making of the claim leads to contempt. But to be slighted is the greatest *animi molestia*, and from the feeling of being slighted arises the greatest will to injure. The one slighted longs for revenge. In order to avenge himself he attacks the other, indifferent whether he loses his life in so doing. Unconcerned as to

---

[9]An animal's desire to mate can also only be satisfied by a member of its own species, but a cat which never has occasion to express or satisfy this desire is still fully a cat.

the preservation of his own life, he desires, however, above all that the other should remain alive; for 'revenge aimeth not at the death, but at the captivity and subjection of an enemy...revenge aimeth at triumph, which over the dead is not'. The struggle which thus breaks out, in which, according to the opinion of both opponents, the object is not the killing but the subjection of the other, of necessity becomes serious, because it is a struggle between bodies, a real struggle. From the beginning of the conflict the two opponents have, without realizing and foreseeing it, completely left the imaginary world. At some point in the conflict, actual injury, or, more accurately, physical pain, arouses a fear for life. Fear moderates anger, puts the sense of being slighted into the background, and transforms the desire for revenge into hatred. The aim of the hater is no longer triumph over the enemy, but his death. The struggle for preeminence, about 'trifles', has become a life-and-death struggle (*PPH*, 20-21).

The attempt to give objective reality to one's vanity leads necessarily to violent death—whether one's own or another's, as chance dictates. But glorying does not in fact correspond to a natural, objective reality:

For if we...consider...how easy a matter it is, even for the weakest man to kill the strongest, there is no reason why any man...should conceive himself made by nature above others. They are equals who can do equal things one against the other; but they who can do the greatest things, namely kill, can do equal things (*De Cive*, I, §3).

Resting on a false opinion and necessarily leading to the greatest human evil, attempts to objectify one's glorious imaginings lack both theoretical and practical justification; they are unconditionally to be condemned.

The situation with respect to the contrary passion, viz., the fear of violent death, is not analogous. It rests on a true opinion concerning one's own power. It *may* lead to violent death, particularly in the state of nature where, for example, to secure oneself one may make a preemptive strike against another. This is an important point, because it shows that the state does not spring naturally from a human passion. But it is easy to see that killing others to preserve oneself is a shortsighted course of action; men being naturally equal, none would be able to survive more than a few such encounters. The most rational way to avoid violent death is to find allies and combine forces with them to face the rest of the world. "It is a precept or general rule of reason that every man ought to endeavor peace as far as he has hope of obtaining it; and when he cannot obtain it, that he may seek and use all helps and advantages of war" (*L*, xiv). The first half of this precept Hobbes calls "the fundamental law of nature," but he later admits that it is not a law in the proper sense of the term: in obeying it we 'obey' only our own passion of fear.

Hobbes himself attached great importance to his starting, unlike the classical thinkers, from the passions. Since they are what truly move men, a political science founded upon them can be expected to prove more solid. At the very beginning of the first exposition of his new doctrine, he tells us that his project is to "put such principles down for a foundation, as passion not mistrusting, may not seek to displace; and afterward to build thereon the truth of cases in the law of nature (which hitherto have been built in the air) by degrees, till the whole be inexpugnable" (*Elements of Law*, Epistle Dedicatory).

G. Some Consequences of Hobbes's Rejection of Classical Rationalism

The link or mediator between the passion of fear and the commonwealth is reason. Reason is thus, if you like, at the basis of political association for both Hobbes and Aristotle—but in wholly different ways. For Aristotle man was necessarily a political animal because naturally endowed with the power of rational speech. According to Hobbes, men institute commonwealths on the basis of a particular rational calculation: that they, generally and for the most part, conduce to self-preservation.

This shift in reason's political function is a consequence of a shift in its anthropological status. In the classical teaching, as we have said, *logos* is the proper guide of the passions; Socrates in the *Republic* called *thymos* its ally, and placed desire below both. For Hobbes, desire is the director of human action, and reason is its subordinate and tool: "the thoughts are to the desires as scouts and spies, to range abroad and find the way to the things desired" (*L*, viii).[10] Glorying, his nearest equivalent to *thymos*, is at the bottom, nearly always requiring to be suppressed.

---

[10]'Thoughts' here clearly refers to practical reasoning. Hobbes does not often use the word 'reason' when referring to action, but in *L*, v, does say that it is by reason we reckon the probable consequences of kinds of events. Presumably such events would include one's own acts.

The reversal of command from reason to desire is, we believe, merely another consequence of the abandonment of teleological anthropology. On the classical account reason's title to rule rested on its ability to discover the objectively valid natural end of human action, or at any rate something closer to it than are the goals most men in fact pursue. Wisdom, which is nothing but the perfect development of *logos*, would be an absolute title to rule. Since no one is in fact wise, the relatively most legitimate political order is based on laws. The purpose of the laws is to guide citizens toward *eudaimonia*; they embody a more or less imperfect understanding of this natural end and adapt it to the citizens' particular situation and vices. They are administered by a specially educated class of noblemen—not philosophers, but men informed, as are the laws themselves, by philosophy.

For Hobbes, there is no greatest good, only various apparent goods and various kinds of power for obtaining them. "The use of laws...is...to direct and keep [people] in such a motion as not to hurt themselves by their own impetuous desires, rashness or indiscretion, as hedges are set up not to stop travelers but to keep them in the way" (*L*, xxx). Laws have nothing to say about their destination; this is determined by the interaction of individual private choices from among the apparent goods and powers which remain licit.

Above we contrasted the Aristotelian view of *pleonexia*, or covetousness, as a vice with the Hobbesian view of it as a necessary consequence of the illimitable character of human desire. It is now easy to see the political consequences of the respective teachings. On the Aristotelian view, laws should keep desire 'within the bounds of reason' by discouraging excessive luxury. In fact, it was something of a commonplace among ancient moralists, not only philosophers, that too much wealth was harmful to both state and citizen. But Hobbes endorses unlimited acquisitiveness: "the public stock...cannot be too great for the public use" (*Behemoth*, in *English Works*, vol. 6, 45). Laws should only restrict the 'how' of acquisition, not the 'how much.' The practical effects of this shift in orientation have been beyond all calculation. Less often understood is its basis in philosophical anthropology.

As for the relation of reason and desire in the context of political power, here is Hobbes's answer to the traditional teaching:

> I know that Aristotle in the first book of his *Politics*, for a foundation of his doctrine, maketh men by nature some more worthy to command, meaning the wiser sort (such as he thought himself to be

for his philosophy), others to serve (meaning those that had strong bodies but were not philosophers as he)—as if master and servant were not introduced by consent of men but by difference of wit, which is not only against reason but also against experience. For there are very few so foolish that had not rather govern themselves than be governed by others; nor when the wise in their own conceit contend by force with them who distrust their own wisdom do they always, or often, or almost at any time get the victory (*L*, xv).

As with Hobbes's 'refutation' of the *finis ultimus*, the most charitable way of interpreting this passage is as polemic—aimed at the popular discrediting of the Aristotelian tradition rather than at explaining the true grounds for Hobbes's own break with it. Formally, the first argument is a begging of the question: title to rule arises from desire rather than reason because the fool does not *desire* to be ruled by the wise man. The second argument does not address wisdom itself, but the subjective feeling of certainty; in so doing it ignores the possibility of Socratic wisdom, that is, the possibility that the propensity to self-doubt is the sign of an unfinished movement toward wisdom.

But the author of *Leviathan* was a sufficiently competent thinker to see the objections to which these arguments were exposed. In our view the real basis for his rejection of rational political legitimation was his new understanding of science and of reason itself. *Logos* had been understood by the ancients as the natural human capacity for grasping general truths about the world as it exists independently of any particular human mind. According to Hobbes, the mind cannot grasp that which is independent of itself. Consider, for example, his explanation of 'science:'

It is science when we know a certain proposed theorem to be true, either by knowledge derived from the causes, or from generation by the subject through right reasoning. On the other hand, when we know (insofar as possible) that such and such a theorem may be true, it is knowledge derived by legitimate reasoning from the experience of effects. Both of these methods of proof are usually called demonstration; the former kind is, however, said to be better than the latter, and rightly; for it is better to know how we can best use present causes than to know the irrevocable past, whatsoever its nature. Therefore science is allowed to men through the former kind of *a priori* demonstration only of those things whose generation depends on the will of men themselves (*De Homine*, x, §4).

In sum, knowledge, insofar as it is not merely hypothetical or conditional, is a kind of making. Whereas for the classics science was primarily concerned with what is necessarily true independently of the will or action of particular men, that is, with *physis*, for Hobbes science is primarily concerned with *techne* and *nomos*, that is, with man's own action and production. As a consequence, there cannot be for Hobbes any unambiguous distinction between theory and practice. This is among the most important innovations of modern thought.

Hobbes proceeds to interpret geometry according to this principle; the famed certainty of this science arises "because we ourselves draw the lines, and the generation of the figures depends on our will." And analogously, "Politics and ethics (that is, the sciences of *just* and *unjust*, of *equity* and *inequity*) can be demonstrated *a priori*; because we ourselves make the principles—that is, the causes of justice, viz., laws and covenants—whereby it is known what *justice* and *equity*, and their opposites *injustice* and *inequity*, are" (*De Homine*, x, §5). So far from making a science of human things impossible, the rejection of a teleologically understood human nature is the precondition for making *nomos* the subject matter of a science as certain and lucid as geometry.

For this reason it is misguided to make Hobbes's mechanistic account of nature, given in *De Corpore*, the basis for interpreting his 'civil' philosophy. Such a procedure can only lead to a naturalistic anthropology. Moreover, Hobbes himself makes clear more than once that politics has its own principles drawn from self-observation and ordinary unscientific experience (*De Cive*, Preface; *De Corpore*, vi, §7; *L*, Introduction). It may even be that his materialistic *Naturphilosophie* was in part designed as a handmaid to his political teaching; surely it is an ideal remedy for that "fear of powers invisible" which he recognized as the most important obstacle to the public acceptance of that teaching. Be that as it may: it is sure that Hobbes regarded politics and morals as a science admitting of certainty, and physics as irremediably hypothetical.

To summarize: Hobbes's standard is derived from nature—not the nature of political association itself (for it has none) but from the natural passion of fear. Fear is not, however, the direct and sufficient cause of commonwealth; otherwise commonwealth would indeed be natural. Prompted by fear and guided by reason, men *institute* commonwealth—or acquiesce, overtly or tacitly, in its institution or continuation.

This institution, rather than its natural motive, provides the standard: that form of government is best which best fulfills the human, contingent purpose for which men establish governments, viz., "the foresight of their own preservation, and of a more contented life thereby" (L, xvii). On this basis Hobbes argues, for example, the superiority of monarchic to aristocratic and democratic rule. We can *know* that he is right about this, that he is not merely expressing a subjective preference, because security and contentment are the aims we all pursue in consenting to the institution or continuation of commonwealth. Commonwealth exists, indeed, by convention—but by one virtually universal, since it is rooted in a natural passion; and we can understand and evaluate it precisely because it is our own product.

Action in a Hobbesian commonwealth may be imagined as a ray—perhaps not a particularly straight one—ever receding from its origin, never reaching anything. That origin is nature, and especially the natural fact of death. Rather than being the good which men approach, nature is the evil which they flee (without ever finally escaping it). As such it provides, if you like, a kind of negative standard: art and convention are good insofar as they help us depart from our natural state. But they do not point us in any particular direction.

This, at any rate, is Hobbes's teaching. We must now determine whether it succeeds in resolving the difficulties which arise from the abandonment of natural teleology.

H.   Difficulties with Hobbes's Teaching

The political teaching of the *Republic* is utopian, and the entire tradition which followed upon it preserves this utopianism to the extent it makes man's perfection the source of its scientific criteria. It was for this reason that Hobbes described previous natural law teachings as "built in the air." He, like Machiavelli before him, desired to orient himself according to man-as-he-is rather than man-as-he-ought-to-be. This 'realism' is the source of both the greatest strengths and the greatest weaknesses of Hobbes's thought, as we shall now see.

Man is dominated by passion rather than reason. Plato and Aristotle granted, even emphasized, that this was and always would be true of 'the many,' though they denied it would be true of the perfect sage; and they held that the sage's rationality could be approached by the philosopher. But according to Hobbes no one can ever be dominated by reason; hence it makes no sense to say that anyone should be. Reason is only effective in the service of some passion.

Since no one is motivated by reason *instead of* passion, reasonableness cannot provide a title to rule. Instead, this title is based on a convention or covenant. By this covenant, Hobbes tells us, men fearing violent death agree to give up their natural right to determine the means of their own preservation: either to one who has power over them (commonwealth by acquisition) or one to whom they choose to grant power over themselves (commonwealth by institution) (*L*, xx).[11] In either case, once the covenant has been made, the *fact* of holding political power is its own sufficient title. As if to illustrate this teaching, Hobbes, after having repeatedly condemned the acts by which parliament wrested power from the king, quietly returned to England from France in 1651 and submitted himself to the usurpers. A rebellion is unjustified only as long as it is unsuccessful; all successful rebellions are legitimate. In the case of sovereignty, fact equals right.[12]

This authoritarianism has some awkward consequences for another aspect of Hobbes's teaching. For he intended that teaching to be practical, expressing the "hope that one time or other this writing of mine may fall into the hands of a sovereign who will...by the exercise of entire sovereignty, in protecting the public teaching of it, convert this truth of speculation into the utility of practice" (*L*, xxxi). Hobbes is forthright in presuming to teach sovereigns their own business. The awkwardness—we shall leave undecided for the moment whether it is a genuine contradiction—is that, by his own account, he has no *right* to do this. Any sovereign, whether wise or foolish, has a perfect right to determine which doctrines are and are not allowed to be taught; he could, therefore, justifiably proscribe Hobbes's works (*L*, xviii). Hobbes says, indeed, that the power to control the public teaching of doctrines should be aimed at the preservation of civil peace, which might seem to be a limitation on the sovereign's authority in the matter. But not so: for, first, the sovereign has a perfect right to choose the means by which public peace is to be preserved; if he chooses foolishly

---

[11]Hobbes prudently refrains from speculating about the basis for the covenanters' choice in the case of commonwealth by institution. This would have to be a natural difference of some sort, which might easily be used as a standard of legitimacy within civil society once instituted, that is, serve to justify rebellion under certain circumstances.

[12]Perhaps elsewhere too—for example, in the state of nature, where no act is unjust, the right of self defense is indistinguishable from the capacity for it. But we must beware generalizing from these cases to an interpretation of the entire Hobbesian teaching as 'what is, is right.' Hobbes distinguishes between rightly and wrongly *motivated* acts both in the state of nature and in commonwealth. 'Iniquitous' is his technical term for what is naturally morally objectionable: see *De Cive*, I, §4; iii, §5; xiv, §18; *L*, xv.

the subjects are still bound by covenant to acquiesce. Second, the sovereign is not even bound by any covenant to pursue civil peace; the subjects covenant with one another to submit to a sovereign for the sake of peace, but they do not covenant with the sovereign himself. Hobbes tacitly assumes that the sovereign will have at least some interest in preserving the peace. Thus, a sovereign would be justified even in proscribing Hobbes's works for their being *too* pacific in spirit. This would obviously be very foolish from the point of view of Hobbes's own thought—but not unjust.

There is thus a tension between Hobbes's 'realism'—the derivation of right from covenant and consequent equating of the right of sovereign power with the fact—and his practical recommendations. To discover the source of this tension we must return once again to his account of the state of nature. "The natural condition of mankind" he describes as "a war of every man against every man." Though perhaps overly familiar, we cannot forebear to quote Hobbes's great description of this war:

> In such condition there is no place for industry because the fruit thereof is uncertain, and consequently no culture of the earth, no navigation nor use of the commodities that may be imported by sea, no commodious building, no instruments of moving and removing such things as require much force, no knowledge of the face of the earth, no account of time, no arts, no letters, no society, and which is worst of all, continual fear and danger of violent death, and the life of man solitary, poor, nasty, brutish and short (*L*, xiii).

On Hobbes's account, natural men are hungry, frightened wretches whose first need is for peace and cooperation. It is not surprising that they do just as he describes: covenant with one another with a view to security and commodiousness. Here, in other words, Hobbes's 'realism' coincides with his recommendations. This is hardly an accident. Indeed, although he claims to be deducing right from what happens in the state of nature, he has rigged his account of that state to yield the principles of right he was aiming at all along. His recommendations are not a consequence of 'realism;' it is rather his 'realism' which has been tailored to fit the recommendations—in other words, it is not genuinely realistic. To demonstrate this let us see what happens if we alter the assumptions about the state of nature.

I.   A Thought Experiment to Bring Out the Ambiguities in Hobbes's
     Teaching

The two most important natural passions, according to Hobbes, are
love of honor and fear of violent death. Whereas Hobbes portrays the
love of honor as hostile to political association as such, the *Republic*
teaches that it is the root of a particular type of regime: 'timocracy.'
This latter view is not at all implausible; it is a matter of verifiable fact
that states which allow considerable scope for the pursuit of honor, at
least on the part of a certain class, have survived, thriven, and
expanded. Hobbes himself is forced to admit, though he does not
emphasize, that love of honor is a useful quality in soldiers. And he
tacitly assumes that, even in a commonwealth where his
recommendations are fully put into effect, enough love of honor will
remain for some men to *want* to exercise or administer sovereign
authority. Finally, as we have already mentioned, the love of honor is a
social passion in the sense that one needs other men to honor one;
'glorying,' which is a kind of imagining, naturally seeks confirmation
of itself, as Hobbes recognizes.

On the basis of these considerations let us assume that the state
comes into being not simply out of the desire for security but out of a
confused mixture of that desire and the love of honor. Some of our
natural men desire honor more than life: they, or such of them as
survive the war of all against all, become the sovereign authority.
Others submit for dear life. Still others submit to seek the lesser honor
of "public ministers of sovereign power" (*L*, xxiii). A state is thus
established allowing a certain amount of room to the different natural
passions of the men who live in it. None of these passions is naturally
legitimate; the question of legitimacy only arises within the state once
constituted. Authority having passed to the sovereign, he has a perfect
right to decide what is just and what unjust. He may even outlaw the
printing of *Leviathan* if he thinks it overly denigrates the pursuit of
honor.

The 'theory of the state' which we have just sketched amounts to
one half of Hobbes's own teaching. Denying that fear of death is
naturally more legitimate than love of honor, we can preserve the
Hobbesian 'realism:' by the covenant, the fact of sovereignty is its
right. But then Hobbes's recommendations are unjustified. His
preference for a commonwealth directed exclusively towards security
and commodious living has no basis in nature or convention. What we
have, in effect, is a political 'science' in the best twentieth-century

fashion: a 'purely descriptive' account of the state, compared with which Hobbes's directives for practice are 'mere value judgments.' A timocracy is no less legitimate than a secure and commodious Hobbesian commonwealth.

Now let us return to the beginning and change the assumptions. Let the love of honor be naturally wrong. Only the desire for security is truly legitimate. Either men institute commonwealth for the sake of security, in which case they are acting rightly, or out of a love of honor, in which case they are acting wrongly. But it is not very important now how the state is in fact instituted; we have an evaluative standard independent of fact. Laws and actions by the sovereign are legitimate insofar as they help achieve, or at least aim at achieving, security and commodious living. The right of sovereignty does not follow from the fact. Timocracy is necessarily illegitimate. Even if all men and states pursue honor, this can never make it right. Since the good and the right are independent of fact, there is no contradiction in saying that all men are bad and all states illegitimate. It is easy to see that what we have here is the other half of Hobbes's teaching: his recommendations without his 'realism.'[13]

But Hobbes wanted to have it both ways—to equate the right of sovereignty with the fact *and* to redefine what a good state should be. In order to do this he had to leave his starting point ambiguous. Sometimes he seems to be deducing right from what men do in fact desire, other times from what they should desire. Is this simply a contradiction?

J.   How Classical Philosophy Could Resolve Hobbes's Difficulties

Not necessarily. Classical philosophy reasoned in the following manner: All men necessarily desire what is good for themselves. Thus, a sick man, desiring health, may equate health with happiness; a poor man, desiring wealth, may think that happiness is wealth; etc. These beliefs are confused and shortsighted, but each grasps a part of the

---

[13]The litmus test for these competing interpretations would be suicide. If violent death provides the standard merely because it is feared, generally and for the most part, suicide would be intrinsically morally indifferent (though perhaps extrinsically unjust if legally prohibited, or iniquitous if, for example, small children are thereby left uncared for). If the standard is based on the natural goodness of life suicide would be intrinsically wrong (though perhaps excusable in certain kinds of circumstances). Hobbes's freedom to express himself on this issue was limited.

truth. Happiness does involve a certain amount of health and wealth; they are necessary but insufficient conditions for *eudaimonia*. According to this teaching there is necessarily some connection between what men do in fact desire and what is rightly desirable: no one, for example, could desire to burn in hell. Everyone may have a false belief about a matter indifferent to anyone's good; there is no contradiction in everybody believing the moon to be made of cheese. But concerning the Good we are at most confused, not wholly mistaken. This is the thought behind Socratic dialectics: the truth about the human things is contained, albeit confusedly, in the opinions of ordinary men, and can be brought out by analysis. There is a connection between the Socratic method and the naturalness of the state, just as Hobbes's basing of the state on a contract is related to his view of knowledge as making.

However that may be—the classical doctrine is teleological; it asserts the primacy of man's true end, and understands the ends men pursue in relation to that naturally determined end. Ignoring for a moment Hobbes's rejection of teleology, we can sketch as follows a parallel interpretation which integrates the descriptive and moral sides of his thought: men in fact pursue both honor and security; the first pursuit is unjustified, since it is based on a purely imaginary superiority over others; the second is justified, corresponding to a true assessment of our power. Insofar as men are enlightened, either by the experience of fear or by the study of the true (Hobbesian) philosophy based on the justifiableness of fear, they cease to be confused; they no longer seek *some* honor and *some* security, but devote themselves single-mindedly to the pursuit of security. Then they approach the secure and commodious commonwealth which is their true end.

On this interpretation *Leviathan* is a work with theoretical and practical purposes similar to Aristotle's *Politics*. It clarifies the true end of human action, the end confusedly pursued by all men at all times: that is its theoretical purpose. And it aids those fortunate enough to understand it, or to live in a state informed by an understanding of it, by clarifying the end of their action: that is its practical purpose. By revealing to men their natural equality and frailty, *Leviathan* helps them to abandon the foolish and destructive striving for honor, to banish timocratic elements from the state, and to establish a secure and commodious commonwealth in accordance with their nature.

This interpretation does, we believe, harmonize the realistic and moralistic aspects of Hobbes's thought. But it is stillborn; it assumes what we know from the outset to be false, viz., that his thought is teleological. We appear to be stuck in a 'trilemma,' if you will: exclusive realism, exclusive moralism, or teleology. All are demonstrably counter to Hobbes's own intentions. The central claim of his philosophy is, as we stated earlier, that the true, nonteleological understanding of man issues not merely in a recounting of what men happen to have instituted up to now, but in an account of what human institution always is and what it always should be. We appear forced to conclude that he failed.

K. How Modern Philosophy Might Resolve the Difficulties without Departing from Hobbes's Own Principles

We see one possible way out of our 'trilemma.' It involves going well beyond anything Hobbes himself ever said, but renders what he did say consistent.

Commentators have often remarked on the contrast between the Hobbesian state of nature and most prephilosophical accounts of the origin of human things, for example, those of the Bible or Hesiod; for the older notion of 'good beginnings' and a subsequent 'fall' the philosopher substitutes 'bad beginnings' and 'progress.' But Hobbes also maintained a goodness of beginnings in one decisive respect: it is in the moment of the commonwealth's establishment that everything *is* as he declares it *should* be, that description and recommendation coincide. The parties to the covenant do exactly as Hobbes would have all subjects do at all times: submit for their survival. As time passes they forget their fear and take political association for granted. Then it is that the antisocial love of honor, disguising itself as love of liberty, comes to the fore; the subjects break their covenant, call their protector a tyrant, and dissolve the commonwealth. The practical usefulness of *Leviathan* Hobbes saw in its *reminding* his fellow subjects of the true origin of the state, of its real, preexisting contractual basis. The secure and commodious commonwealth he recommends is thus not intended to be something radically new; it is simply a logical extension of the original covenant.

We have already made our criticism—and it is by now an old criticism—of Hobbes's procedure: it is a begging of the question, in that it tailors the account of the state's origin to suit the political recommendations the philosopher wishes to make independently of any such account. But this criticism is valid only because the state of nature and ensuing covenant are hypothetical reconstructions of the past—or, if one rejects the historical interpretation, of the anthropology logically anterior to politics. Either way the coincidence of description and recommendation was asserted by Hobbes to hold *prior to* the imperfections of existing states.

Let us see what happens if we construct a state in accordance with Hobbesian principles, leaving aside the question of whether or not this is a return to the 'true beginnings' of political association. Hobbes himself never tried to describe the state that embodied his recommendations. One of the most important consequences of his doctrine is never explicitly drawn in his own writings: its perfect embodiment requires world government. As long as separate commonwealths exist the state of war remains actual between them (see *L*, xxx, towards the end). If art and convention are unequivocally superior to nature, that is, if commonwealth is always preferable to the state of nature, this state should be left completely behind. That can only happen when a world state is established. How this might come about is a question of secondary importance: conquest would be as effective and legitimate as institution. For "the rights and consequences of...*despotical* dominion," that is, commonwealth by acquisition, are "the very same with those of a sovereign by institution, and for the same reasons" (*L*, xx). The philosopher of 'peace at any price' is not squeamish about what that price may be: he provides an implicit justification for world conquest.[14]

Let a world state be established, then, and let a copy of *Leviathan* "fall into the hands" of the sovereign. He does all in his power to suppress the pursuit of honor and encourage that of security and comfort. He commands the public teaching of Hobbes's works in all universities. From every pulpit the people are taught that the "powers invisible" regard meek and faithful subjects kindly and direct their wrath against the proud. The armies of old become a simple police force. It is possible that in these circumstances people would in fact begin to see themselves as Hobbes portrayed them; they might

---

[14]This follows, for example, from *L*, xi, and the "general inclination of all mankind, a restless desire for power after power." Kings are men; hence "kings, whose power is greatest, turn their endeavors to the assuring it at home by laws or abroad by wars." To say that kings ought never to do this is to say that they ought not to be human. Peace is possible, and often prudent; but men being what they are, it always remains more or less a mere truce.

eventually forget what 'honor' ever meant and focus exclusively on enjoyment and on securing the way to future enjoyment. Such a society does not entirely exceed our imagination.

Now let us ask which of our possible Hobbes interpretations fits this world state. Is Hobbism functioning here as a doctrine concerning the 'true' end of man, justifying the aims of the world sovereign? Or is it merely a descriptive, 'unevaluative' account of what passions men have in point of fact, and of how they go about satisfying them? It is hard to know just what to say. We are confronted with a single reality; a society's beliefs about what it *should* be are, after all, a part of what it *is*. As with Hobbes's 'original covenant,' description and justification coincide. The difference between this world state and the Hobbesian covenant is that the covenant was held to be historically or logically preexistent, the *basis* for subsequent action; whereas the world state is the *product* of human action, without necessarily having any counterpart in nature or earlier history.

This, we believe, is the only way the contradiction between the realistic and moralistic aspects of Hobbes's teaching can be resolved without implicitly or explicitly restoring natural teleology: by realizing the state he recommends. At present, in other words, Hobbesian morality is not 'realistic,' and to say it should be realized means, if it means anything, that it is man's true or natural end. At present, Hobbes's doctrine is contradictory, that is, necessarily false; but, if actualized in a world state, it could become true. In other words, it might be *made* true.

It is possible to understand Hobbes's writings as a sort of high-order propaganda aimed at helping to bring about the state he advocated. This is admittedly not Hobbes's own understanding of what he was doing. He spoke of "converting this truth of speculation into the utility of practice." He believed his political teaching already true because he believed the human passions had, at the historical or logical origin of political association, been in fact as they should always be thereafter—and had been bound by covenant to remain. If we reject this thesis for the reasons explained above, Hobbes's 'truth for the guidance of practice' becomes a project, a subjective ideal without natural or historical support, which might become true at some future time. The practical function of his writings would not be, like that of Aristotle's *Politics*, to enlighten men as to their natural *telos*, but to form other men's wills in accordance with the author's own, to impel them toward the end he has set. Hobbes's philosophy would not be a representation of reality from which certain practical consequences follow; it would be itself a political act.

Such a reinterpretation of the Hobbesian project would even bring a certain epistemic advantage from Hobbes's own point of view. For in his explanation of 'science' quoted above, he admits the irremediably hypothetical character of all inferences from effects to causes. And of course his political teaching rests on just such a reconstruction of the remote causes of commonwealths. But if his project is actually carried out we will obtain perfect *a priori* knowledge of his principles. Theory and practice—knowledge and action—are, for the consistent philosophical 'modern,' inseparable. The publication of Hobbes's doctrine was perhaps itself the first step toward the establishment of a new and greater Leviathan: "for the actions of men proceed from their opinions, and in the well governing of opinions consisteth the well governing of men's actions" (*L*, xviii). Hobbes was perhaps the heir of Lycurgus, Romulus, and Moses no less than of Socrates, Plato, and Aristotle.

Of course, the timid philosopher of Malmesbury, "the first of all that fled" the English Civil War, was not himself a world-conqueror. And there is no necessity about the establishment of the secure and commodious world state; if it were understood as necessary we would be driven back to a 'naturalistic anthropology' and *Leviathan* would be a theory of physics. Hobbes's project may never be fully realized, in which case its contradictions are real and his theory of the state simply false. The lacuna in his thought, the gap between description and recommendation, could only be filled by human, contingent, 'unnatural' actions—by war and political fiat—by future history.

L.   Carrying the Modern Project Forward

Hobbes's was the first distinctively modern anthropology—the first which, basing itself on man 'as he is' rather than man 'as he should become,' tried to establish standards for understanding and evaluating the human things. In discussing his teaching we have turned up two sources of confusion. One is the discrepancy between what we have been calling the 'early' and 'late' states of nature. The other is the conflict between 'realism' and 'moralism,' or description and recommendation. These two gaps in Hobbes's thought have something important in common: both call for a kind of history. In the former case we require one to explain how man passed from the early state of nature, in which he was merely an animal with an ability to 'inquire consequences,' to the late state in which he was already capable of speech, reason, covenants, and the like. Rousseau made the first attempt to write it, in his *Discourse on the Origin of Inequality*. The second gap, between observed passions and objective standards of conduct, was more difficult, requiring as it did a *future* history. Hegel was the philosopher who made the most important attempt to fill it.

We shall try to demonstrate in what follows that Hegelianism is the completion—that is, both culmination and end—of the modern project. The question of the success of this project is, we assert, simply identical to the question of the truth of some form of Hegelianism. And since it is impossible within modern thought clearly to separate theory and practice, the truth of Hegelianism is anything but an 'academic' question. It may be no extravagance to say that "the future of the world, and therefore the sense of the present and the significance of the past, depend in the last analysis on the manner in which one interprets today the Hegelian writings" (Kojève, *HMC*, 365-366 =Eng. 42).

III. THE FOUNDATIONS OF A HISTORICIST ANTHROPOLOGY

A. Kojève's Modern Understanding of Nature

Kojève's principle exposition of his version of Hegelianism takes the form of an interpretation of the *Phenomenology of Spirit*. On his view, that work is "a philosophical anthropology, independently of what Hegel may think" (*ILH*, 39). For this reason he attributes particular importance to chapter IV, A of that work—the famous passage concerning the struggle for recognition, in which humanity first emerges. It is in his interpretation of this story that we find the source of most of his characteristic doctrines and themes. But to appreciate the significance of the 'anthropogenic struggle,' we must know something about what precedes it.

The first three chapters of the *Phenomenology* are devoted to what Kojève calls 'external-consciousness' or 'contemplation.' Although meant to represent the lowest rungs on the ladder to absolute knowledge, these chapters contain some abstruse material: chapter three, for example, alludes to Newtonian mechanics and Kant's speculative philosophy. The transition that occurs in chapter four is thus not from the 'simple' to the 'complex' as we ordinarily understand the terms.

What is common to all mere external-consciousness, distinguishing it from even the lowest manifestations of animal life, is *inertness*. The Newtonian observes, but does not act upon, the planets whose motion he calculates. One may object that a man who remains inert will never learn to contemplate the heavens in the manner of Sir Isaac Newton. This is true, of course; the natural sciences are a form of human *activity*, and as such they are considered in chapter five, after the emergence of man. But scientific activity is supposed merely to prepare the scientist for the correct, passive apprehension of a naturally 'given' object; that object is itself conceived as remaining unaffected by its observation. In this regard a system of celestial mechanics is no different from the naive sense-certainty of *Phenomenology*, chapter one, expressed in such utterances as 'here is a house' or 'now is daytime.' In both cases an object is conceived as what is preeminently real, true or concrete. But in fact it is an abstraction, only real as part of a relation; a human subject is always present. The scientist may believe that to abstract from his own existence is to cling to something 'higher'—an eternal natural order, or even the visible manifestation of God. But since man and the natural world have no real separate existence, it would be more accurate to say that in and by the scientific activity of man the world becomes conscious of itself (*ILH*, 454 and note =*IRH*, 177 and note). The 'truth' of external-consciousness is self-consciousness, and self-consciousness is always human. Or, to put it less grandly, Newton is better than the planets, since no planet could have written the *Principia*.

Strauss, in his book on Hobbes, suggested that the modern break with the classical tradition might be epitomized by the contrast between Hobbes's statement that man is "the most excellent work of nature" and Aristotle's that man is "not the finest thing" in the cosmos.[1] On this point Hegelianism is certainly a 'modern' teaching. Hegel remarked that not only men but even animals transcend contemplation of the 'given,' viz., when they set to and eat it up.[2] Kojève, in a similar vein, writes that "the man absorbed by the object he contemplates can only be 'brought to himself' by a Desire, for example, the desire to eat" (*ILH*, 11 =*IRH*, 3).[3]

Natural desire, introduced by Hegel at the beginning of chapter four before the struggle for recognition, is active rather than inert. The subject no longer stands apart from the object. A bear *goes* in search of prey, *catches* it, *devours* and thus *transforms* it. In Hegelian jargon,

---

[1]*PPH*, 35. The passages he cites are: *Leviathan*, Introduction; *NE*, VI, 1141a21.

[2]*PG*, ¶109 (citations will be by paragraph number to facilitate reference to the English translation by Arnold V. Miller).

[3]It is noteworthy that Kojève does not, as one might have expected, contrast the lack of desire in inanimate things with the desires of animals; instead he speaks of contemplation by a human and the occurrence of a natural desire in a human. In doing so he is following Hegel's phenomenological method. We cannot know 'what it is like' to be a stone, nor even to be *merely* an animal, but these levels of being reveal themselves in and to man through such experiences as silent contemplation and hunger. To simplify our own presentation we shall usually speak directly of things, animals and people. Kojève would call this a 'metaphysical' rather than 'phenomenological' account.

desire 'negates' its object. But it does not negate or transform the subject. On the contrary, the consequence of the satisfaction of natural desire for the subject is merely an extension of itself in time, that is, survival. In other words, the negating of the object amounts to a 'positing' of the subject: feeding and mating, animals assert themselves within the natural order. One might even say that animals, in desiring to feed and mate, 'desire to survive;' at least, their natural, desire-driven activity involves a certain self-awareness absent from pure contemplation. Kojève calls this a 'feeling' or 'sentiment of self.' Human self-*consciousness*, which is discursive self-awareness, is a development—a humanization—of the animal's feeling of self.

Before humanity emerges, the world has these two fundamental or irreducible aspects: natural things and natural desires. It is important to understand that those aspects do not coincide with the classes of inanimate and animate beings. An animal is also a thing, a body composed of the same elements found in inorganic nature. There are things without desires, but no disembodied desires. The dividing line between things and desires runs, so to speak, through the animal itself. A desire is a lack of something. Kojève calls it "the presence of an absence" (*ILH*, 367 =*IRH*, 134; also *PD*, 237). In a celebrated passage he compares it to the hole in a ring. The hole is a kind of nonbeing; it *is* where the ring *is not*. But this does not mean that there 'is not' a hole. If there were not, the ring would no longer be a ring. But it would still *be*—it would be a disc, or a lump of metal, or whatever. On the other hand, the hole could not exist in any sense without the ring. Take away the ring, and the hole is not transformed: it simply disappears. In other words, the hole is an aspect rather than a part of the ring; it is separable only in discourse. Analogously, desire is a negative aspect, a kind of nonbeing within the animal: thirst, for example, is a lack of water (*ILH*, 487n).[4] Apart from the body of the animal, desire is literally nothing. But an animal which cannot desire anything is dead, that is, no longer an animal in the primary sense. In speaking of desire we must beware the temptation to reify it, to treat it as a 'thing' within animals; but we must also bear in mind that it is a constituent of the animal qua animal, that is, it is an *essential* aspect.

B. The Source of Kojèvian Humanity

To speak as we just have of animal desire 'negating' its object may cause a misunderstanding. Negation being a well-known Hegelian term, it may appear that Kojève's understanding of animal nature as well as of humanity is importantly different from that of classical philosophy. In fact, Aristotle was already perfectly familiar with *this* kind of negation.[5] Animal negation partakes of the cyclical character of natural life in general: the animal 'negates'—kills and devours—its prey in order to maintain itself. Animal life is a series of naturally occurring desires for natural objects, the attainment of which tends to the preservation of individual or species; on this point there is no quarrel between classical and Hegelian thought. But for Kojève there is also a specifically human type of negation which brings forth something new rather than merely preserving what already exists. The essential difference between classical and Hegelian thought falls, according to Kojève, within the domain of anthropology.[6]

The ultimate source of human negation, and therefore of humanity itself, is an 'unnatural' desire— the 'desire for recognition.' Kojève defines it as a desire not directed at any object, but rather at another desire. The reader will look in vain for this specific difference of man in the writings of Hegel. In his private correspondence, Kojève admitted:

> ...as concerns my theory of the desire of desire, it is not in Hegel either, and I am not sure he saw the matter well. I introduced this notion because I had the intention of making, not a commentary on the *Phenomenology*, but an *interpretation*; in other words, I tried to recover the basic premises of the Hegelian doctrine and to construct it by deducing it logically from those premises. The 'desire of desire' seems to me to be one of the fundamental premises in question (letter to Tran-Duc-Thao, 7 October 1948; quoted in Auffret, 249).

What it means to 'desire desire' can be clarified by a comparison of erotic love with animal sexuality. An animal's (including *Homo*

---

[4]The *sensation* of thirst and its connection with the lack of water which is 'thirst' in the primary sense is a separate problem which the ring analogy does not pretend to resolve: see *ILH*, 368n1 =*IRH*, 135n1.
[5]Kojève states that Aristotle's account of the biological realm can be inserted without change into the Hegelian system: *EHRPP*, vol. 2, 312 bottom.
[6]This is not so clear in Hegel's own writings. Kojève rejects Hegel's philosophy of nature.

sapiens') desire to mate is triggered by positive natural traits or behavior in combination with its own metabolism. But a mere animal cannot, for example, be jealous or experience romantic longings. In other words, everything which makes up animal sexuality is also found in erotic love, but not conversely. And according to Kojève, the basis of all which is specifically human about love is a 'second-order' desire. "The Desire is only human if the one does not desire the body but the Desire of the other, if he wants to 'possess' or 'assimilate' the Desire qua Desire, that is, if he wants to be 'desired' or 'loved' or better still, 'recognized' in his human worth, in his individual human reality" (*ILH*, 13 =*IRH*, 6).[7] Furthermore, the desire which is the object of a human desire is itself not merely natural; a lover does not want to be desired only as a means of satisfying a sexual or unerotic desire.[8] This is the source of the specifically human phenomenon of shame or modesty.

The example of eroticism may mislead one into understanding the 'desire to be desired' in too narrow a sense. It is present equally in the desire for certain things: "the Desire for a natural object is only human insofar as it is 'mediated' by someone else's Desire for the same object.... Thus, an object perfectly useless from a biological point of view (such as a medal or the enemy's flag) can be desired because it is the object of others' desires" (*ILH*, 13 =*IRH*, 6). In the human world to 'possess' something is to have it 'belong' to you, to be a 'part' of you in a broad sense. So to possess something desired by others, such as a flag, is to be oneself an object of their human desire—even, or especially, if they are trying to kill you in order to dispossess you.

Or again, money is something desired exclusively because other human beings desire it: it ceases to be 'money' in the strict sense as soon as no one any longer wants it. It is thus preeminently human or nonnatural. It is significant in this regard that money was for the ancients the paradigmatic case of something that exists by convention: the word *nomos* is related to the word for 'coinage,' *nomisma*. An anthropology which makes the desire for desire the source of humanity as such is thus a quite radical form of conventionalism, of the ancient 'unclassical' tradition represented by the sophists and Democritus.

---

[7]In fact, a slight misstatement. Kojève means '*insofar as* one does not desire...' or 'if one does not *merely* desire....' He is not speaking of so-called platonic love.

[8]Thus Kojève in one place calls human desire "the Desire which aims at a Desire *aiming at a Desire*" (*ILH*, 169 =*IRH*, 41; our italics). This explains, incidentally, why recognizing the humanity of others is a precondition of satisfying one's own human desire, that is, why the satisfaction of second-order desire can only be reciprocal.

Finally, let us consider how human desire operates in politics. A man wants the state of which he is a member to adopt a certain course of action. This necessarily implies that he wants other citizens to want the same. Where desires regard the body no such conclusion follows: someone who likes eating snails may well prefer that no one else should, so he can have all the snails to himself. But where desires regard the human community to which one belongs they must also regard the desires of the other members. Because, first of all, no one can put his political ideas into effect by the use of natural force. The strength of one man is at most great enough to subdue one or two of his fellows, but in no case the entire state. Even a dictator requires others who agree with him or sincerely accept his authority if he is to carry out his wishes (see *OT*, 144). But secondly, the use of force is in any case a *pis aller*. For example, a law punishing murder and a police force to thwart murderers are merely the best substitutes available for no one desiring to commit murder in the first place, that is, for everyone sharing the desire of those who established the law and the police. Someone who says he desires that no murders be committed or that institutions be established to prevent and punish murder, but who also claims to be indifferent as to whether *anyone* shares these desires, thereby contradicts himself.[9] Either his 'desire' is a mere dream or fancy, or he does not understand that a community of desires is the basis of human community as such. 'Value relativism' is incoherent.

There are several ways of acting on political desires. In the case of *force*, from terrorism to legal punishment, others are led to act according to the political agent's desires through fear, that is, they 'desire' what he desires in preference to personal harm or death. In the case of *authority* they desire what the agent desires because he is the one desiring it, independently of the consequences to themselves from acting on the desire. In the case of *persuasion* they are drawn to the desire of the agent (become a speaker) by its content, without regard to his person or office. But the common basis of all these modes of political action is the assimilation of the desires of others to the agent's own.

These few examples—erotic, military, economic and political—should help to make clear the meaning and some of the explanatory power of the 'desire of desire.' It is in fact closely analogous to the animal's desire for food. Just as the latter prompts the assimilation of a

---

[9]"What is it to *realize*, to objectify one's ideal if not to get it recognized by *others*, by *all* others?" (*ILH*, 204).

natural object to the animal's natural being (its body), so the former prompts the assimilation of the desires of others to one's own 'nonnatural being' (one's human desires). Recognition is another name for this assimilation. And since one's nonnatural desires are one's humanity (*in posse*), the desire to assimilate the desires of others amounts to a desire to have one's humanity recognized. Kojève is thus justified in using the expressions 'desire of desire' and 'desire for recognition' interchangeably.

Characterizing certain types of behavior as specifically human must not be confused with asserting them to be *entirely* human. People desire wealth partly as a means to satisfying animal needs and wants; erotic love includes a merely sexual aspect, etc. Nothing in Kojève's teaching denies the possibility of what is now called sociobiology. In an interview given shortly before his death, he said, "that [the human sciences] recognize in man a space where something other than humanity functions, that is normal. In man there is one percent that is human and the rest is, let us say, animal."[10] But it is the special task of philosophy, as opposed to the empirical sciences, to render an account of this essential one percent.

C.   Kojève and Hobbes vs. the Classical Teaching

The desire for recognition is for Kojève man's irreducible specific difference, corresponding to the 'ability to inquire consequences' in Hobbes. It is the source of all which is not the product of nature or chance—in other words, of all art and convention, all the human things.

Nature, we recall, is that which comes before art and convention and remains unaffected by them. A tree is natural; a table is the product of art, but cannot exist without a natural basis, viz., wood. A newborn is natural; a magistrate is the result of a law or convention, but also has a natural basis. This would include at least—as with the table—his 'matter,' his flesh and blood. It is the task of philosophical anthropology to discover what else may be natural to human beings, what is the product of that mixture of custom, art and chance called 'education,' and, most especially, what is the human *source* of art and convention.

---

[10]*Interview*; compare *PD*, 486n. "One percent" is, of course, a metaphor; humanity is a qualitative aspect, not a discrete quantity.

There are two ways to go about responding to these questions that we may eliminate at the outset. The first consists in identifying some ordinary natural trait, not different in kind from those found in the rest of the animal kingdom, as man's specific difference: for example, some peculiarity of his brain structure. That is then asserted to be (perhaps in interaction with other biological or environmental factors) a sufficient condition for the arts, convention, speech and all that is human. This is what we have called 'naturalistic anthropology.' It involves, as we said, the implausible notion that nothing human is essentially different from the rest of nature. But the decisive objection is that, as has often been pointed out, it is incapable *in principle* of accounting for itself as knowledge. The brain structure theory, for example, is by its own report a natural effect of the formulator's brain structure—as would be any argument against it. Naturalists must either refuse to see this or be reduced to groundless assertion ('My brain structure is producing true belief, yours false'). In either case they place themselves outside the bounds of a *philosophical* investigation.

Alternatively, we might want to say that no natural facts—whether internal or environmental, whether separately or in combination—could ever provide a sufficient explanation of the human things. And we can, if we like, cover the gap in our understanding with an impressive name such as 'free will' or 'spontaneity' or 'creativity.' The consequence is still that man cannot be the object of timeless, universal, scientific knowledge. If naturalism does away with the 'anthropo-' of anthropology, spontaneity deprives us of the '-logy.'

The classical solution, as we have seen, was to identify *logos* as man's most important specific difference: speech and reason, understood as the ability to grasp truths, and those truths understood to include the 'true good for man.' The classical tradition usually allowed that man may have other specific differences not reducible to *logos*, for example, the 'spiritedness' introduced in the *Republic* and maintained by Aristotle. Classical philosophy is not 'naturalistic' in our sense, since *logos* differs essentially from anything found in the animal kingdom, and not merely as one birdcall differs from another. Yet *logos* is, or is part of, a *human* nature. It is permanent, not 'invented' by anyone, and not altered by anything man can do. Socrates' *logoi*, or speeches, may be better than a fool's, or than his own as a child, but the natural human power of speech is identical in all cases. *Logos* underlies particular *logoi* somewhat as natural materials do the products of human art. Furthermore, man's true good, which is aimed at and hence presupposed by all human acts, is 'given' by nature. No one can *make* cowardice, stupidity or disease good; man does not 'posit values.' *Logos* allows us to *discover*, partially and imperfectly, what our good is. And since that good is the naturally determined end or purpose of all our actions, everything necessary to attain it is natural (that is, humanly natural): political society, education, the arts, and even that development of *logos* itself which is called 'philosophy.'[11] Speech, reason, the good, man's purpose, truth, the city, human nature—all these are inseparable on the classical account. If they are not always seen to be in harmony, this is due to human imperfection.

The modern project is to account for the human things and provide evaluative standards to guide human action without having recourse to the classical doctrine that the essential truth about man and the Good for him are naturally 'given' and merely discovered by reason. Hobbes was the founder of modern anthropology so defined, and Kojève's Hegelianism is, so we shall argue, its fulfillment. The differences between their teachings are important, and we shall try to clarify them in the rest of this chapter. But now we want to look at their common 'modern' starting point.

Both Hobbes and Kojève, in setting forth their candidates for man's specific difference, are concerned to find something which can be the source of all other human things. They cannot, obviously, pick something which is itself conventional or artificial. It must, then, be something natural.[12] But it cannot be an ordinary, 'given' natural trait. And it cannot be a natural end, nor speech understood as naturally directed to revealing such an end.

Their solution is to identify a potentiality as man's specific difference. The *ability* to inquire consequences, the *desire* for recognition—neither is, by itself, anything at all *in acto*. The actual things arising out of them make up the nonnatural or human world. The paradox of human nature, that it amounts to a 'non-nature nature'—the same paradox resolved in the classical tradition by teleology—is here resolved by the distinction between potency and act. Man's nature, one might say, is to be potentially not merely natural.

Of course, classical thought does not claim that *logos* is ever fully actualized, that is, that anyone is ever perfectly wise and good. So the defining principle of its anthropology is also a kind of potentiality. But classical thought involves what might be called a 'realist'

---

[11]Not *nomos*, however. Where man's end is attained, in a perfect city ruled by wisdom, laws and customs are replaced by knowledge of the good.

[12]Chance is another logical possibility, but that would yield the pseudo-anthropology of free will or spontaneity.

understanding of potentiality. The true and the good are supposed to be effective in human beings at all times, informing and calling forth their thoughts and acts. Nothing comes from nothing; what leads man to transcend a merely animal existence must therefore itself have some sort of existence—'ideal' or 'divine,' let us say. All human speech, convention and art is an approximation to it.

Hobbes's response to the classical teaching has already been discussed. Kojève, too, rejects it lock, stock and barrel:

> It can be said that Work is carried out according to a preconceived Idea or a Project: the real is transformed according to the ideal. But the Idea is only *a priori* in relation to the effective and effected Work and not to the Man who works: it is not an 'innate' or 'platonic' Idea. Man *creates* the idea by ideally creating the (natural or social) given, and he *realizes* the Idea by effectively inserting it in the given by the Work which really transforms this given according to the Idea. The evolution of means of transportation, for example, was not carried out according to the 'idea' or 'ideal' of the automobile, an 'idea' given in advance and gradually approached by successive efforts. Man started by having himself carried by other men or by animals solely because he no longer wanted to walk 'naturally,' that is, on foot. And it is by *negating* successively the different means of transportation which were first *given* him that he finally produced the automobile, which is a true creation not only as a material object but also as an 'idea', which did not 'preexist from all eternity,' neither in man nor elsewhere (*ILH*, 500n =*IRH*, 229n).[13]

Human desire, for Kojève, differs from natural desire not by being directed at 'higher,' divine or ideal things, but at *nothing*—at a desire, an absence, a felt lack in others. Its apparent satisfaction—being loved, capturing the enemy's flag, piling up money—does not destroy the desire, but merely transforms or redistributes it. Hence, for Kojève as for Hobbes, the action prompted by human desire is linear *in principle*, and not simply because it never in fact attains its true object.

Farther than this modern anthropology cannot go. One may, of course, ask whence such an indeterminate potentiality arose in the natural world: is it connected with some type of brain structure after all? Perhaps. Indeed, there is no reason not to admit that it must have

---

[13]What Kojève says here of work he means to apply equally to all human action.

some genetic, and therefore natural, precondition.[14] But no genetic pattern need *be* the potentiality in question. The lack of such identity is enough to distinguish Kojève's (or Hobbes's) doctrine of man from all forms of naturalistic anthropology.

D. Kojève vs. Hobbes

The attentive reader may have noticed that our explanation of human desire in Section B is, as it stands, circular. We said that the desire for recognition seeks to assimilate the human desires of others to one's own. But this supposes an already humanized world. And the world is humanized by action and discourse arising *from* human desire. To take an example: it may indeed be human to show off a new diamond ring. But that merely leads us to the more fundamental anthropological questions of how people came to place a value on naturally worthless stones, how arts such as gem-cutting arose, and how a legal system was established recognizing ownership of objects of desire such as diamonds. In a word, we must return to the 'state of nature' and see how human desire is *first* actualized. Then we may begin to explain how its continuing operation in a humanized world takes on diverse forms and produces the human things as we observe them.

For Kojève, the original 'anthropogenic act' was none other than the 'mortal struggle for pure prestige' described in chapter IV, A of Hegel's *Phenomenology*. And because in his view "the description of the 'phenomenal' dialectics of human existence...is Hegel's principle title to glory" (*ILH*, 490 =*IRH*, 218), he uses this passage in which humanity emerges as a kind of key for interpreting the entire Hegelian philosophy.

The desire for recognition, we said above, is the functional equivalent within Kojève's anthropology of Hobbes's 'ability to inquire consequences.' But it *resembles* quite a different Hobbesian concept: glorying. Hegel's 'unmediated self-consciousness,' like the man in Hobbes's late state of nature, imagines himself superior to all others. In Hegel's own words, "self-consciousness is at first simple being-for-itself.... Its essence and absolute object is *I*.... That which is other for it exists [only] as an inessential object marked with the character of the

---

[14]"We allow that [the desire of desire] can only appear in a representative of the animal species *Homo sapiens*" (*PD*, 237). But such desire cannot be deduced from the nature of that animal.

negative" (*PG*, ¶186). And, like the glorier, Hegelian 'natural man' cannot rest content with his private thoughts; he "is only as [he is] recognized" (*PG*, ¶178). Of course, the other natural men are of no mind to grant such recognition. This is one reason the first action motivated by human desire can only be a struggle.

But the origin of humanity in struggle is more than an accident of circumstance. As Kojève explains:

> For man to be truly human, for him to differ essentially and really from the animal, his human Desire must effectively overcome the animal Desire in him. The supreme value for the animal is its animal life. All the animal's Desires are in the final analysis a function of the desire it has to preserve its life. So human Desire must overcome this desire for preservation. In other words, man only 'proves himself' human if he risks his (animal) life because of his human Desire. It is in and by this risk that human reality creates and reveals itself (*ILH*, 14 =*IRH*, 6-7; see also *PD*, 240).

Man emerges only from a reciprocal interaction. The glorying and demand for recognition on the part of one nascent human being provide the risk which permits human desire to prove its effective superiority to animal desire in the other. In other words, humanity is essentially social: "there is nothing human outside of Society, since man only becomes a human by becoming a social being, and vice-versa" (*PD*, 182).[15]

Aristotle, too, held that man abstracted from his social relations is not human in the primary sense:

> The city is prior by nature to the household and to each of us. For the whole must of necessity be prior to the part; for if the whole [body] is destroyed there will not be a foot or a hand, unless in the sense that the term is similar (as when one speaks of a hand made of stone), but the thing itself will be defective. Everything is defined by its task and its power.... If the individual when separated [from the city] is not self-sufficient, he will be in a condition similar to that of the other parts in relation to the whole. One who is incapable of participating

---

[15]See also *ILH*, 13 =*IRH*, 6: "man can only appear on Earth within a herd." The solitary life of anchorites is a poor objection: no one is born an anchorite. The human aspect of such a way of life, for example, the idea of service to a divinity, depends on previous socialization.

It does not appear to us that such a doctrine of the origin of humanity would commit one to 'collectivism' as an ideal for the future of man. In general, origins are not authoritative for the historicist.

or who is in need of nothing through being self-sufficient is no part of
a city, and so is either a beast or a god (*Politics*, I, 1253a19-29).

In other words, man and city cannot exist separately because part
and whole share a common natural purpose. For Kojève, by contrast,
man and society are inseparable because they originate as
complementary aspects of the same unnatural interaction. There is a
certain analogy between the two teachings, but this is due to their
diametrically opposed orientations.

Hobbes also tried to reverse the Aristotelian teaching. He did so,
however, not only by rejecting man's natural-social purpose, but also
by making humanity prior to political society in the chain of *efficient*
causes. The covenant instituting commonwealth is made by beings
who, as he tells us, speak, live in family groups, fear gods and glory in
imagined superiority to one another—in other words, by *human* beings.
Kojève's teaching (which follows Hegel following Rousseau's *Second
Discourse*) is that these human traits, while not 'political' in a narrow
sense, are as much the result of nonnatural human interaction as the
institution of a sovereign. Kojève derives society—and not merely
sovereignty—along with all human traits from an animal nature with an
'unnatural' potential (corresponding to Hobbes's early state of nature).
In other words, Kojève renders more consistent and thoroughgoing the
conventionalism of modern anthropology by eliminating the late,
already human state of nature.

Kojève and Hobbes appear to differ also in their evaluation of the
effects of rivalry or the pursuit of honor. Rejecting what he took to be
Aristotle's doctrine that "man is a creature born fit for society" (*De
Cive*, I, §2),[16] Hobbes asserted the universality and quasi-naturalness of
the apparently antisocial passion of glorying, which "maketh men
invade...for reputation." Kojève, by contrast, makes the desire for
recognition the very foundation of society. But a closer look reveals
that this difference is more rhetorical than real. For, first of all, we must
bear in mind that Hobbes's glorying *is* a social passion in the sense that
it is necessarily directed at others of one's species. It is only antisocial
in the sense of being potentially disruptive of the peace of the

---

[16]Once again a misrepresentation of Aristotle's views. Two of the eight
books of the *Politics* are devoted to the function of education in the city. If
man's nature is his end one may sensibly speak of a 'natural education'
directed to that end. Such an education will indeed be necessary to render a
man "fit for society." But once again, there can be no doubt that Hobbes
rejected the genuine Aristotelian teaching as well as his caricature of it.

commonwealth. Kojève would certainly agree on both points. Secondly, in his account of 'commonwealth by acquisition' Hobbes allows us to see, though he does not wish to draw attention to, the way in which the pursuit of honor can contribute to the establishment of civil peace (for example, in *L*, xx). And this is one of the main points made by Hegel's story of Master and Slave. In short, Hobbes passes over the political and human usefulness of rivalry as nearly as possible in silence, while Kojève tends to emphasize it. But both teach 'man's unsocial sociability;' both are opposed to the earlier doctrine of his naturally determined social purpose.

But, as we know, there is a real difference beneath the rhetorical one: while Kojève teaches that the desire for recognition is the deepest source of all which is human, Hobbes held that glorying is derived (somehow) from a more fundamental potential—that of inquiring consequences. In other words, the pursuit of honor is a contingent fact. There could have been, and with proper political action might one day yet be, a *human* world from which that pursuit is absent. For Kojève this is simply impossible: inquiring consequences (that is, *techne*) is necessarily posterior to the struggle for recognition prompted by glorying. From a Hegelian point of view, Hobbes's error was to believe slavery—that is, work and the arts—to be possible before or apart from mastery. This is *the* substantive disagreement between them. For the rest, Kojève mostly renders consistent, clarifies and completes the Hobbesian project.

E.   A Philosophy of Freedom

The capacity for accepting risk, manifested in the struggle for recognition, is the original form of human *freedom*.

An animal's desire is for natural objects. Although desire is an absence, a lack of—or, if you like, a 'freedom from'—its object, such an absence or 'freedom' is *determined* by the object desired; it is itself a natural desire. So animals, whose irreducible specific difference is natural desire, are a function of the things they desire: a part of nature, partaking of its unchanging character. The only purpose of their behavior is the extension of their natural being in time, that is, continued life and reproduction. (This purpose is, moreover, not self-conscious—not, therefore, a 'purpose' in the human sense; animals do not *plan* to feed and mate).

Man, by contrast, creates himself qua man by manifesting independence of his natural being, risking his life. And he does so out of a desire for another desire, something immaterial, 'unnatural.' Insofar as he risks his life he is no longer a function of nature and cannot be explained merely by referring to natural things or qualities (whether in him or outside of him).

Kojève's teaching concerning freedom must be distinguished from traditional notions like free will or spontaneity. As he puts it, "freedom does not consist in a *choice* between two givens; it is the *negation* of the given" (*ILH*, 494 =*IRH*, 222). The paradigmatic case of human freedom is not a traveler arrived at a fork in the road but a soldier ready to act against his natural desire for self-preservation because of a principle, an idea. But such an idea is not 'given;' it is unreal unless and until human action realizes it. And such action is not carried out in virtue of some 'given' quality or faculty of the human soul outside the natural domain. In Kojève's words, "freedom is not a property; it is an act" (*ILH*, 65-66).

Free human action negates X, that is, makes it into a 'not-X.' But the action and the 'not' are not ineffable or ideal or divine entities 'mixing' with the X. Apart from it they do not exist. But in it, they *do*: not-X is not 'pure negation,' but something as real as X was—a Y, in fact. It is essentially different from X, but it exists because the X of which it is the negation existed. If freedom provides the 'not,' nature provides the 'X.' If freedom makes the human world *what* it is, nature assures *that* it is. If freedom is like the hole which makes the ring a ring, nature is like the matter of the ring which allows there to 'be' a hole.

The prehegelian doctrine of free will eliminates, explicitly or implicitly, the possibility of anthropology, of universal and timeless knowledge concerning the human things. For Kojève, on the other hand, nature is an unchanging element upon which human freedom always acts, and which makes that freedom a determinate and knowable reality.[17] In other words, it assigns humanity a fixed starting point. Of course, if anthropology is truly to be timeless knowledge there must also be a fixed endpoint. If that endpoint is a naturally determined 'ideal,' a 'human nature' which it is the eternal task of humans merely to realize and not to create, then we have a classical anthropology. But then man is not genuinely independent of all that is

---

[17]Hegel himself points out that this determinacy of negation is what distinguishes his philosophy of freedom from ordinary scepticism: *PG*, ¶79; compare *ILH*, 477-478 =*IRH*, 203-204.

given, not free in Kojève's sense. On his view, man creates ideas or projects from *nothing*, from his nonnatural desire, and then freely realizes them through action. If such a doctrine of human freedom is to be embodied in an anthropo*logy*, a timeless scientific account, it must include a description of the actual—not merely ideal—end of human action. This is why Hobbes's unclassical anthropology remains a mere project and his practical recommendations lack any real foundation. But of this more later.

Nonnatural desire is Kojève's way of accounting for human freedom; but in another sense, of course, freedom is precisely what cannot be accounted for: free acts are not subject to the principle of sufficient reason. These two senses of 'account for' correspond, respectively, to Hegel's German terms *erklären* and *ergründen*. We explain the possibility of risking one's life by citing a nonnatural desire—that is an *Erklärung*. But we cannot deduce the struggle, or its outcome, from the desire—that would be an *Ergründung*. It is instead the desire which we infer from the fact of struggle. For human desire is pure potentiality; it has no reality apart from its actualization. Man's action is free in the primary sense; his desire is so in a derived sense. The phenomenologist writes, and can only write, after the free and unpredictable action is complete. For him it is a 'given,' an observation rather than an inference, a starting-point for his investigation (see *ILH*, 168 =*IRH*, 39 top). There could be no crasser misunderstanding of Hegelian historicism than as an *a priori* deduction, *à la* Spinoza, of 'laws of the historical process.'

The emphasis upon freedom in Hegelian philosophy appears to distinguish it from Hobbism. Hobbes's scorn for the *liberum arbitrium* of the schoolmen is well-known. But a closer look reveals that, here too, the would-be materialist prefigured Hegel. Hobbes was aware that an uncompromising mechanistic monism is inherently unable to account for itself as discourse. This is what may have inspired his revolutionary doctrine of 'knowing is making.' He had to find a domain safe from mechanical causation, even if only to write his *De Corpore*; the world of human construction (or 'creativity') was that domain. *Nomos* is independent of *physis*, civil philosophy of natural. This independence could just as easily be called freedom. It is no solution to the problem of free-will as traditionally conceived (that is, the fork in the road)—neither is the Hegelian doctrine. But perhaps that merely means that human freedom has traditionally been misconceived. Hobbes's remark that freedom of the will was not an 'error' but an 'absurdity' seems to indicate that he thought so (*L*, v).

It is sometimes said that the ancients were unaware of the problem of 'metaphysical freedom,' and it is true that there is no expression in Plato or Aristotle which could be correctly translated 'free will.' But it is also true that classical thought allowed that there was an essential difference between man and the other animals, evidenced by purposive artistic and customary action. And since such action varies over space and time, it cannot be merely naturally determined animal behavior. Whether the nonnatural realm of art and convention deserves to be called free depends upon how its existence is explained.

We have seen that the fundamental specific difference of man on the classical account is *logos*. The question, therefore, boils down to whether rationality, as classically understood, allows for freedom. Kojève answers that it does not.

Rationality, as classically understood, includes the ability to apprehend truth. Truth is increate and eternal, no less where it concerns man than elsewhere. And it is practical: it can determine action ('virtue is knowledge'). The sage, the imaginary man in whom reason is perfectly developed, would therefore be determined in all his actions by knowledge of the good. Insofar as two sages' actions differed, it would be due to differences in their circumstances (including their own bodies). There is no 'freedom from truth' except error, which in the practical realm is called vice.

Apparently nonnatural human action is determined in part by the true good for man (insofar as he perceives it), and in part by irrational human passions (*thymos,* etc.). But even these last appear to be part of an inalterable human nature: the education of the passions must recommence with each generation. In a word, human vacillation between rational, passionate and animal behavior is caused by the interplay of various natural forces (or by chance) rather than by any 'freedom' from them in the Hegelian sense. The case is analogous to the interpretation of political change as occurring around fixed points.

But, granting that Hegelian thought can account for freedom better than classical thought, what happens to the classical doctrine of the eternal character of truth?

F.   Freedom and Truth

Hegel says of the glorying consciousness preceding the struggle for recognition that "its self-certainty still has no truth, for its truth would be only of its own being-for-itself presented itself to itself as an independent object" (*PG*, ¶186). This means first of all that human desire drives man to seek confirmation of private self-certainty from others—an idea familiar to us already from our discussion of Hobbes. But we are apt to be perplexed by Hegel's use of the word 'truth.' It is tempting to interpret his words as a colorful way of saying that the glorier cannot *know* before the struggle whether his subjective certainty corresponds to reality. This would be a grave error: Hegel means literally that a statement of self-certainty preceding the struggle can be neither true nor false. For only the struggle itself creates a reality for such a statement to correspond to. *This is the fundamental principle of historicism.* Insofar as the struggle is human it is not a test of strength, nor the revelation of any preexisting natural fact, but the creation of a new nonnatural or human fact,[18] a new 'truth' in the proper sense of the word. As Kojève says:

> Man cannot grasp himself consciously before the objectivizing Action because there is *nothing* in him which might be known. Before the Action he is only Desire or *pure* Ego, that is, a *void* which only becomes something one may know by the active negation of what *is* and of what is *not* it: of *Sein*, of the given. For Man *is* his activity; he does not *exist* outside his work [*œuvre*]. And *that* is why he can only grasp himself consciously by relating to himself as an object, relating to his *work*, the *product* of his action (*ILH*, 227.) [19]

In a word, there is no 'true self' *behind* our acts—merely a desire, a kind of nonbeing.

One might respond that the same goes for animals: there is (presumably) no 'true dog,' but only a desire, behind such canine behavior as feeding and mating. Yet dogs do not 'create truths,' do not essentially alter the world with their behavior. Kojève's response would be that natural desire is directed at presently 'given' objects; but that nonnatural desire, being unsatisfiable by anything 'given,' must take the form of a plan, a project. That is why it can create something that has never before existed, such as a new kind of machine or political

---

[18]"The equality...of the anthropogenic Struggle has nothing to do...with physiological or natural equality, being merely an equality of human conditions" (*PD*, 254). *A fortiori* of the inequality following the 'unnatural' struggle.

[19] Among the prehegelian teachings rejected in this passage are: the Christian (and Kantian) doctrine of conscience, Rousseau's natural man buried underneath the perversions wrought by society, and the teleological notion that action is an attempt to live up to a preexisting ideal (Pindar's "become what you are!").

system. Glorying is a belief or subjective certainty which, while not true, becomes a plan of action and hence does alter the objective order of things. If the emergence of Master and Slave is the first revolution in human history, the subjective certainty of the Master might be called its 'ideology;' and we can apply the following words of Kojève, written with a later historical period in mind, to the struggle for recognition:

> What is an ideology? It *is* not a *Wahrheit* (an objective truth), nor an error, but something which can *become* true by the Struggle and Work which will put the World in conformity with the ideal. The test of Struggle and Work renders an ideology true or false. We notice that at the end of the revolutionary process what is realized is not the ideology pure and simple from which we started, but something different, which is [its] truth ('revealed *reality*') (*ILH*, 117).

The situation following the struggle for recognition is objectively real, but it cannot be adequately accounted for by referring only to the real, outward situation of the two *Homo sapiens* preceding it. It is also, and essentially, the result of a subjective certainty, a project. Man is a planning animal.[20] So an adequate anthropology must be 'teleological'—at least in the etymological sense. It must render an account (*logos*) of purpose (*telos*) in human action. Otherwise it will be—in fact if not by intention—naturalistic.

What distinguishes classical anthropology is thus not the idea of purpose *per se*. It is rather that of *natural* purpose: the teaching that the plans embodied in human action are apprehensions of a preexisting idea (the good, human wellbeing, justice, or something similar). The classical doctrine is epitomized by Aristotle's inference that since all acts aim at some good there must be a 'good'—ideal yet natural—at which they aim. On Kojève's view, this is barely preferable to subphilosophical naturalism:

> This supposed Man of the ancient tradition is in fact a purely natural (=identical) being who has neither freedom (=Negativity) nor history.... And if he differs essentially from the animal it is solely by his thought or coherent discourse (*Logos*), whose appearance in the Cosmos, moreover, was never explained. But this Discourse negates nothing and creates nothing: it contents itself with revealing the given

---

[20]Thus one cannot admire (recognize) a person for unintentional behavior: it is not genuinely human. Similarly, it is possible to love an infant or pet, but not to esteem it. And in the last analysis this is because it cannot plan what it does.

real (error remaining in fact inexplicable). So Discourse, that is, Man, is a part of [*fait corps avec*] Given-being (*ILH*, 535; *IDPH*, 119-120).[21]

In a private letter to Strauss, Kojève went so far as to draw a connection between the classical teaching and Nazi biologism (*OT*, 262)!

However that may be, the basis of the classical teaching is the belief that human action, being real, must have a real source: nothing can come from nothing. Kojève, on the contrary, sees the distinguishing feature of human existence precisely in its creation of something—a machine, a social institution—out of a 'nothing,' a nonnatural desire: "The profound basis of Hegelian anthropology is formed by the idea that Man is not a Being...but a Nonbeing [*Néant*] which negates [*néantit*]...by the...transformation of the given starting from an idea or ideal which *is not* yet, which is still nonbeing ('project')—by the negation which is called *Action*" (*ILH*, 175 =*IRH*, 48 top).

A consequence of this is that for Kojève, in contrast to the classics, an ideal or a plan *only* has reality insofar as it is realized by action. So, although man is *essentially* a planning animal—meaning that a being with no capacity for acting with a view to the future would not be what we call 'human'—a merely planning and dreaming *Homo sapiens* would not be *actually* distinct from the rest of nature. Only the struggle itself is truly anthropogenic, not the private self-certainty which prompts it. Kojève could not, consistently with his own principles, have produced a *Republic*, a discursive utopia claiming *truth*.

G. Atheism and Mortality

The authority of nature as a norm and the eternal character of truth are not all that modern man is required to sacrifice on the altar of his own freedom. Theism and the doctrine of immortality are incompatible with the carrying out of Hobbes's project.

Kojève offers the following definition of 'divine being:'

> A is *divine* in relation to B and for B (that is, for the consciousness B has of him) if A is supposed to be able to act on B without B being

---

[21]*EHRPP*, thirteen-hundred pages long, is in large part a development of the assertions made in this passage.

able to react on A.... Example: as long as men believed the stars acted on them but that they could not act on the stars, these were considered divine; but since physics has revealed to us that the action of the stars on us is exactly equal to our reaction on them, they have been "secularized" (*PD*, 34 and note).

It is obvious that 'nature,' as understood by classical philosophy, is divine in this sense. The rejection of God, as we shall see, follows the same reasoning as the rejection of the classical teaching. Modern thought is inherently atheistic.

According to Kojève, "the fundamental principle of all Theism whatsoever" is that

the Evil is the Not-good without the Good being the Not-evil.... Whence it follows, first, that one cannot be aware of an evil or imperfection unless one knew *already* what the corresponding perfection or good was, and second, that by improving something one merely reestablishes it in the state it was in *before* having deteriorated.... Thus, for example, it is not because cavemen perceived that a wood-fire heated them very imperfectly that we have central heating today. [Rather,] they noticed the insufficiency of the wood-fire because they had the notion of an ideal heater.... If the best heater in the world is still imperfect today, if it has always been so and if it will never be perfect, this is because the ideal heater is from before [*en deçà de*] the Past itself or beyond the Future as such.... [It] is outside of Time....

Undoubtedly the example of the ideal heater sounds like a bad joke. But it suffices to suppress the *heater* while keeping the *ideal* to obtain the unique Principle from which flows all Theism (*EHRPP*, vol. 2, 62-63).

This passage is a counterpart to the one quoted above in Section C (p. 56). There it was a question of human action, and nothing was said about God, but here we see that for Kojève these issues are inseparable. Elsewhere he speaks of a "Platonic-Aristotelian tendency...towards the Good *or towards God*,"[22] implying that atheism is merely another side of the modern rejection of classical philosophy. (This may also serve as an *apologia* for our apparently cursory treatment of so fundamental an issue.)

Hegelian thought has the character it does, says Kojève, "because it tries to account for the phenomenon of Freedom, or, what is the same

---

[22]"Kojève-Fessard Documents," 189 (our italics).

thing, of Action" (*ILH*, 482 =*IRH*, 209 top). Now, we all know that the coexistence of human freedom and divine omnipotence is a 'mystery' for the theologian. In fact, says Kojève, it is a simple contradiction. If any being exists who (or which) is divine in relation to man, then man is dependent upon it. Furthermore, the existence of divine power is not compatible with different degrees of divine influence. To speak of the divinity 'allowing' man to do such-and-such is a purely verbal subterfuge—this 'allowance' is, as far as the man is concerned, no different from any other divine act. If there is a God, then wherever man seems to act, he is in reality passive. For example, divine grace and the act of conversion, which "cooperate" in Paul's view, "are in reality incompatible" (*ILH*, 263; see also 346n2). Conversely, if man does freely act, there can be no God.[23]

Making man the free author of his own acts and saying he is constituted by those very acts amounts, in fact, to calling *him* a *causa sui*. To say he creates himself as a distinct being in opposition to nature is to make him in some sense 'supernatural.' To assert that there is nothing to be known but what man has made is to allow man a sort of omniscience. Kojève does not flinch: Hegelian philosophy, he says, is "anthropotheism" (*ILH*, 211 and elsewhere). "Everything Christian theology says is absolutely true provided it is applied not to an imaginary transcendent God, but to...Man" (*ILH*, 572-573; *IDPH*, 154).[24]

One prerogative of divinity is, however, denied the new god—immortality. Once again, this is bound up with human freedom.

> Aristotle already saw that a "possibility" which *never* actualized or realized itself...would in fact be an absolute *impossibility*. So if a being...were to last *eternally* and did not realize certain possibilities...those possibilities would be impossibilities for it.... In other words, it would be rigorously *determined* by these impossibilities.... It would not truly be *free*. By existing *eternally*, a being necessarily realizes *all* its possibilities.... The *given* set of these possibilities...constitutes its immutable "essence," its eternal "nature," innate "character," platonic "idea," etc., which it can

---

[23]This argument is independent of the question of Hegel's personal beliefs. Kojève does attempt to show, however, that Hegel himself was a perfectly self-conscious atheist: see *ILH*, 198-202; *HMC* 345-346 =*IRH*, 25-26.

[24]Of course, 'Man' does not refer to that abstraction the 'human individual.' No man ever existed (sc.: from birth to death) outside society. It is the "*real*, collective, historical man, or, if you will, the State" which "reveals itself to itself in and by a *Religion*" (*ILH*, 200).

develop in time by realizing and "manifesting" it, but which it can neither modify nor destroy (*ILH,* 518-519 =*IRH,* 249).[25]

This does not imply that any being which must die is thereby free. An animal can realize all its essential, naturally given possibilities in a single life, and the life of its offspring is essentially the same as its own. A man, on the other hand, "always dies prematurely in some sense," (*ILH,* 525 =*IRH,* 256 bottom) and each human generation carries forward the work of the previous one. Moreover, says Kojève, the reasoning of Epicurus may properly be applied to animals: while they *are,* death *is not,* so death effectively does not exist *for* them (*ILH,* 524n =*IRH,* 255n). Essential to the anthropogenic struggle is the *conscious* risk of life; man becomes self-conscious in becoming conscious of his finitude. Hence the poignancy of human existence. This is well-illustrated by Homer's *Iliad,* where the lives of men have the high seriousness of tragedy, and the Olympian gods are merely comic—especially when they appear to 'struggle.'

At one point Kojève goes so far as to say that "the acceptance without reservation of the fact of death...is the ultimate source of the whole of Hegelian thought, which merely draws all the consequences, even the most remote, from the existence of this fact" (*ILH,* 540; *IDPH,* 124). And he attaches similar weight to atheism, which he regards as inseparable from mortality (see *ILH,* 538-539 =*IDPH,* 123-124; *HMC* 348 =Eng. 28). But he also emphasizes the gulf which separates a philosophically serious atheism from the attitude of our 'enlightened' contemporaries: "God and the afterlife have always been denied by certain men. But Hegel is the first to have attempted a complete *philosophy* which is atheistic and finitist with regard to Man.... Since Hegel, atheism has never again been raised to the metaphysical and ontological level" (*ILH,* 527n =*IRH,* 259n).[26]

H. From the Anthropological Source to the Actual Beginning of Humanity

The struggle for recognition occurs as follows: two self-certain potentially human *Homo sapiens* meet, one somehow manifests his

---

[25]A few lines below this passage, Kojève approvingly cites Calvin; the doctrine of predestination is the ineluctable destination of the consistent Christian theologian.

[26]He goes on to make a partial exception for Heidegger.

private certainty of superiority to the other, and the other sees it is no different from his own. He sees himself *in* the first; he is outside or 'beside' himself. And he loses his own self-certainty, becomes 'unsure of himself.' To regain his lost self-certainty he must suppress—not necessarily the other but—the *otherness* of the other, that is, he must force the other to recognize his own (earlier) self-certainty. As in the Hobbesian dispute over 'trifles,' the parties begin by aiming at "triumph, which over the dead is not." But, also as in Hobbes, the 'imaginary' dispute about honor inevitably becomes a life-or-death struggle, because it is a dispute between natural beings, between bodies. Each combatant attempts to suppress the other altogether.

If the desire for recognition were a human *nature* necessarily overriding animal desires in man, humans would fight until only one remained on earth. And, as Kojève remarks, this one would be not a whit advanced by all his victories, having killed everyone who might have recognized him (*ILH*, 170).[27] In other words, life-or-death struggle may manifest humanity or independence of animal nature, but by itself it is incapable of realizing a human world. It is possible, however, for a human freely to side with his animal life and against his human desire. This is essentially different from an animal's instinctive fear of predators: the animal has no desire which conflicts with its nature, hence no freedom to behave differently (*ILH*, 54; *HMC* 353 =*IRH*, 32 top).

We may represent the struggle graphically. Let X represent a *Homo sapiens*, H the human desire for recognition and N animal nature. Private self-certainty may be diagramed as follows:

$$X(H)$$

$$X(N)$$

The arrow represents negation, and is dotted to show that it is still merely potential. By contrast, the actualized Master (M) and Slave (S) can be diagramed thus:

---

[27]There are, I am told, forms of animal behavior which resemble the 'natural mastery' Kojève envisions here: for example, queen bees instinctively fight to the death with other queen bees.

M(H)

S(N)

Once again a comparison with classical thought may be helpful. The doctrine that all men share a 'human nature' is not necessarily egalitarian; it is perfectly compatible with the assertion of naturally determined distinctions within the race (whether between individuals or classes). In particular, Aristotle asserted that the distinction between Master and Slave is 'given,' effective from before birth, independent of and unalterable by human action. The laws (*nomoi*) of a state could give slaves equality with or even superiority to their natural masters, but such a state would necessarily be bad. Socrates' 'noble lie' concerning golden, silver, bronze and iron souls seems to be a figure for some similar doctrine.[28]

The Hegelian teaching, derived in this point from Rousseau, is that men are naturally equal—that is, equal on an animal level, as *Homo sapiens* (*ILH*, 403 top)—but not naturally *men*. Inequality and humanity come to be at the same time: when *Homo sapiens* first negates its own natural being. There is no such thing as a *simply* human being *ab origine*, not to speak of a 'human equality.' Man can only emerge in a dual and unequal form.

The human inequality following the struggle is real. The Master is superior to the Slave not only in his private thoughts (as he was before the struggle) but also in the thoughts of the Slave and in their interaction. He gives orders to the Slave and not the other way around—that is an objectively verifiable fact. Yet the fact has been created, not merely revealed, by the free actions of the combatants; it is not a 'fact of nature.' It is, in short, a *nomos*: true because held, considered so, or in Hegel's terminology, *recognized*. Recognition is thus a kind of Hegelian functional equivalent of *nomos*. But the concepts are not interchangeable. A *nomos*, as the ancients knew, implies human beings who hold or recognize it. Hegel made the more radical assertion that humanity itself is in the first instance nothing but

---

[28]*Politics*, I, 1254a18-1255a3; *Republic*, III, 415a. Compare *ILH*, 496 (=*IRH*, 224-225) and *EHRPP*, vol. 2, 331-335. Aristotle's teaching of 'slavery by nature' distinguishes masters from slaves with reference to *logos* which, as we have said, is essentially different from animal nature. It is thus not part of any naturalistic anthropology. Kojève points out that *Phenomenology* V, A, c: 'Physiognomy and Phrenology,' is implicitly a critique of all such doctrines (*ILH*, 82).

the capacity for such recognition: *Der Mensch* ist *Anerkennen.*[29] There is no precedent for this in classical thought.

But it is also important to note that recognition is not, for Hegel, primarily a matter of words. The state is not based upon a compact, as Hobbes asserted; the social contract is rather the discursive expression of what might be called the pattern of effectual recognition in the state. And that pattern is the product of human *action.* In Hegel's words: "language, explanations, promising are not recognition, for language is merely an ideal middle term [between men, that is, in the first instance, between Master and Slave]; it disappears as it appears; it is not a real, lasting recognition."[30]

I.   The Impasse of Mastery

The Master, it seems, has satisfied his human desire. He has proved his superiority to natural being by risking his life for the sake of a nonnatural idea or 'certainty.' He is recognized as 'supernatural,' so to speak, by his former opponent. And since that opponent is now a Slave, the Master no longer has to make an effort to satisfy his natural needs. The Slave transforms nature to accord with the Master's desire.But this human satisfaction is an illusion—for at least three reasons. First, we all know that people are only pleased with recognition from those they respect.

So it is with the Master. But in order to obtain recognition from his opponent he has had to make a Slave out of him. And he regards the Slave as no better than an animal. So the Slave's recognition is of no value to him. In other words, the Master cannot, while remaining a Master, satisfy the human desire for which he risked his life. Mastery is a dead end.

Secondly, the Master's humanity consists essentially in his willingness to accept risk, that is, the *possibility* of death. Until he dies in battle he has not realized his human possibility.[31] And of course,

---

[29]From the Jena lectures of 1805-06; cited by Kojève in *ILH,* 467 =*IRH,* 192; also in *PJ*24 0.

[30]Also from the Jena lectures of 1805-06. For once Hegel makes the point more clearly than Kojève, but we do find the latter saying "this recognition is an action and not merely something known" (*ILH,* 52).

[31]His death is not what we have called 'pure' potentiality (and hence unreal on Kojève's principles), because his objective behavior is affected by it; he risks his life without any biological need. But the living Master has not, by

after he dies he is no longer a human *being*. In other words, the Master's struggle can *manifest* humanity, but not *realize* a human world.

Thirdly, the Master's life, while he is not busy risking it, is concerned with enjoyment—enjoyment of the products of the Slave's work. This way of life is not, indeed, purely natural: animals are not voluptuaries. But its human aspect is not the Master's doing. The Master's eating, for example, differs from an animal's feeding only insofar as the Slave has prepared or denatured his food for him. Everything human in the Master's life, as opposed to his death, is the Slave's doing: "he undergoes a sort of training at the hands of the Slave" (*ILH*, 500 =*IRH*, 229). However many delights mastery gives him to enjoy, it can never make him satisfied with *himself*, satisfied through his own human action.

The unsatisfying character of mastery from the 'inside,' that is, for the Master himself, translates into a historical sterility when it is viewed from the 'outside' by the phenomenologist:

> The risk of life is always and everywhere the same. It is the fact of risk which counts, and it matters little whether a stone ax or a machine gun is involved. Moreover, it is not the Struggle as such, the risk of life, but *Work* which one day produces a machine gun.... The purely warlike attitude of the Master does not vary through the ages, and so *it* cannot be what brings about a historical change. Without the Slave's Work the 'first' Struggle would reproduce itself indefinitely.... The World would remain self-identical; it would be Nature and not a historical, human world (*ILH*, 178 =*IRH*, 51).[32]

J.   The Advantage of Slavery

Slavery begins in mortal fear, which is a necessary counterpart in Hegelian anthropology to the Master's glory. If the Master was correct to see in himself a superiority to animal nature the Slave is also correct to see the vanity, the nothingness of that superiority. For humanity is not a spiritual substance or soul attached to natural being, but a

---

definition, actualized the possibility of death *as such*; in this sense he is still *in posse*.

[32]Kojève would not deny that real wars have brought about real transformations, but would insist that they have only done so insofar as waged for some 'cause' other than a mere desire for mastery. Such causes always involve an element of slavish 'ideology.'

negation of that being. Without the Master's vanity man would not become human, but without the Slave's fearfulness he would very quickly not *be* at all.

The Slave, then, submits himself to the Master, freely inhibiting or 'negating' his own human desire for recognition. The Master's glory is thus transformed into authority and the Slave's fearfulness into service. Service is a kind of conventionalized desire: the Slave agrees to desire whatever the Master desires, or at any rate to act like it. It is thus service which creates that community of desires which is the basis of every association between human beings. For Kojève as for Hobbes, the Slave is the true founder of the commonwealth.

It should be clear from this that our first diagram of the situation following the struggle, viz.,

is in need of revision. It depicts, in fact, the Master's view of the situation. The Slave does not genuinely become an animal by agreeing to be so treated. He continues to desire recognition and is capable of further free human action. Only, his humanity will now take a different form from the Master's unmediated desire for recognition. For example, he may seek recognition from a 'god,' an imaginary divine Master. The situation may accordingly be depicted thus:

The Slave has several advantages over his Master, corresponding to the reasons for the sterile and humanly unsatisfying character of mastery. First, having recognized the human dignity of the Master, he has provided himself with a worthy judge. If he can obtain recognition from the Master it will satisfy his human desire.

Secondly, the Slave's work brings forth a new reality, a lasting human world. Instead of simply destroying his animal nature, the actualization of the Slave's humanity *transforms* nature—both his own and that which is external to him. For example, he fells a tree, hews it, and uses the wood to make a table. Something essentially new has come to be; the 'essence' of the table—that for which we call it a table—is not the same as the essence of a tree. Making a table is thus, if you like, an act of creation. But not *ex nihilo*: it is instead the transformation of a tree. The Slave destroys the tree qua tree, that is, negates its natural form. But he does not add any *thing* to it, for there is nothing in the table which did not come from the tree (or some other natural object). Work humanizes nature but cannot exist apart from it. In Hegelian jargon, human work 'negates' the 'immediate' form of the tree and 'preserves and raises up' its matter in the 'mediated totality' of the table.

Work is, moreover, a negation of the animal nature of the Slave himself. He must do violence to his instincts, inhibit his natural desires, in order to produce 'unnatural' things for the Master. This transforms and humanizes the Slave. No animal makes tables. So when the Slave does so, or at least when he first does so,[33] he is also making himself into a 'table maker,' a type of human being. As Kojève says:

> These two negations are in reality one and the same. To negate the natural or social world dialectically is to negate while conserving it, to transform it; and then one must change oneself to adapt to it or else perish. Conversely, to negate oneself while remaining in existence is to change the face of the World, since it then involves a modified constituent element.... Man...transforms the natural and social World by his negating action, and himself in accordance with that transformation; or, what is the same thing, he transforms the World in consequence of an active self-negation of his animal or social 'inborn nature.' (*ILH*, 494 =*IRH*, 222; see also *ILH*, 179 top =*IRH*, 51 bottom).[34]

The Slave can create a lasting human reality because work is a *mediating* form of negation. The Master may negate his natural existence, but he does so *en bloc*, all at once, and without trying to change anything particular about it. He disappears entirely the moment his humanity is actualized, and the rest of the world is left as it was.

---

[33]Kojève apparently has nothing to say about the important distinction between ingenuity or invention and merely routine work. He definitely means to include the former as a *kind* of work, often using inventions as illustrations: see, for example, *ILH*, 500-501 =*IRH*, 229-230.

[34]The last line should instead say something like 'inborn animal nature or given social reality.'

The Slave 'negates' or inhibits particular natural inclinations for a certain time, as he carries out his work. And he negates particular aspects of the external world, so that a humanized product remains after his action. As Hegel would say, work is 'the negation which subsumes so as to *keep* what is subsumed' (paraphrased from *PG*, ¶188).

By transforming nature the Slave comes to understand and dominate it, and this is the third advantage he has over his Master. The Master's life, as we have seen, is one of enjoyment. But it is thereby less than human. An animal, too, devotes its life to the satisfaction of its natural desires. That is why it is a function of the things it desires. The Master is human, but only 'passively' so, only through his Slave. He depends on the Slave as the animal depends on nature; he is a kind of 'slave to his Slave.' And it is the Slave who, by accepting the Master's uneducated self-understanding and thereby rendering it conventionally true, has deprived him of any desire to transcend it.

But the Slave himself acts according to desires not his own. Hence he is not a 'slave of his desires;' he liberates himself from his animal nature. And this is as much as to say that he ceases to be a *mere* Slave, since the Slave is by definition the one who, in the struggle, was unable to abstract from his natural being. While the Master does not actively change, the Slave comes into being only in order to become something else. Work, the Hegelian equivalent of *techne*, is the source of the historical or 'linear' change observed by the phenomenologist:

> The Man who works *transforms* given Nature. So if he repeats his act he does so under *different* conditions and his act will itself be different. After having produced the first ax man can use it to produce a second which will thereby be different, better. Production transforms the means of production; modification of the means simplifies production; etc. So where there is Work there is necessarily change, progress, historical evolution (*ILH*, 178 =*IRH*, 51).

The Slave in his many forms is thus the true agent of history. The Master by contrast is a kind of catalyst. But it is important to note that the process cannot occur without such a catalyst. "Work is always 'forced' work: Man must...do violence to his 'nature.' And, at least at the beginning, it is another who forces him to it" (*ILH*, 499 =*IRH*, 227; see also *ILH*, 171 =*IRH*, 42). Later on man learns to work for an imaginary divine or internalized Master. And in the end he may work purely rationally: "If he is truly conscious of himself, the Man who has created an artificial World *knows* he can only live there by living (also) as a worker. That is why Man can *want* to continue to work even after having ceased to be a Slave: he can become a free Worker" (*ILH*, 501n =*IRH*, 230n).[35]

To believe that rational work is possible from the beginning, or—what comes to the same thing—that there can be Slaves with no Masters, was Hobbes's most fundamental error (imitated and aggravated by his successor John Locke). It appears first in his anthropological teaching where he says that the inquiring of consequences—leading to the control of nature through efficient causes—is prior to glorying, the source of the struggle for mastery. And it is glimpsed in his political teaching where he seems to hold that commonwealth by institution is just as possible as commonwealth by acquisition *ab origine*. Kojève would surely agree with Rousseau's caustic observation that Hobbes and Locke described how *philosophers*, rather than natural men, would behave in the state of nature.

K.   How Mastery and Slavery Account for Human Motivation

According to Kojève, the desire for recognition which motivates the original struggle remains the underlying motive of human action throughout history: it is "the first and the only truly human Desire" (*ILH*, 126 bottom). This appears to be an unflattering view of the human race. Each man not only attaches an absolute worth to himself and his human desires, but also tries to act as a kind of missionary for himself. As I strive to inculcate my desires or personal authority on others, they are exclusively concerned with converting me to their own. Humanity would appear to be a capacity for engaging in red-faced shouting matches (leaving aside—shall we say—'nondiscursive' ways of producing conviction). But this kind of second-order desire, which we sketched in Section B, corresponds only to the element of mastery in Hegel's story. It seeks to assimilate the desires of others without one's own thereby being affected. This is the more primitive form of human desire. Thus we observe that uneducated and simpleminded people are the least disposed to be dissatisfied with their moral or political or religious convictions, or to empathize with the doubts of others concerning them. The assimilation of human desires, however, need by no means be brought about by the conversion of others; it may

---

[35]The free worker's 'Master' is the state: see *ILH*, 190 =*IRH*, 64-65.

equally result from one's conversion to theirs. This is the element of slavery in human desire. It involves the ability to check one's own unmediated 'self-certainty' and learn from others. It is what permits the embodiment of a general desire in a conventional human community. And only insofar as this element remains effective in the community so established can it continue to change and enact a history.

Kojève's teaching that the desire for recognition is the sole fundamental human desire must not, therefore, be confused with the notion that all human acts are directly motivated by such desire—that the 'honest' man merely wants the reputation for honesty, the arts exist only to make artists famous, etc. In lieu of struggle or propaganda or place-seeking, one may seek to 'impose' recognition through genuine worthiness of it. And the being upon which one seeks to 'impose' oneself may be a god (who cannot be fooled by appearances) or one's own conscience or 'better self.' Kojève by no means denies the reality of moral autonomy or conscientiousness as taught in Christian and Kantian ethics;[36] He merely insists that it is always a mediated form of the original desire:

> One acts only in accordance with a duty one *recognizes*. But the duty one recognizes oneself is always supposed to be recognized by others, who must also, by definition, recognize the worth of him who acts in conformity with this duty. To want to act in accordance with duty is thus in fact to want to have oneself "recognized." But one may not perceive this; one may *think* of the duty without *thinking* of the "recognition." Often, the being who is supposed to "recognize" him who acts "out of duty" is God. Thus one can *believe* that when acting one wants to be "recognized" by God alone. But in fact "God" is merely the "social milieu" substantialized and projected into the beyond. It sometimes *seems* that one does one's duty only so as not to fall short in one's own eyes. But this again is merely an illusion. In this case there is a doubling of individuality into its two components: the one who act represents the Particularity of the agent; the one who judges him "morally" represents his Universality, that is, the social aspect of his existence; the man judges his own "particular" actions in accordance with the "universal" values admitted by the society of

---

[36]"Experience shows that one can...be 'virtuous' without witness (human or even divine) simply out of fear of falling short in one's own eyes" (*OT*, 161).
This is a verbal, but only verbal, contradiction of the next passage quoted. In *OT* he was distinguishing his position from that of a crude reduction of all human action to the desire for recognition, but in *ILH* from Kant's total separation of duty and desire.

which he is part. Of course, one may not recognize the values
"admitted." But if one takes one's "non-conformism" seriously, that
is, realizes it through action, one transforms or wants to transform the
given society precisely so as to have it admit the values for whose
sake one acts. So here again one acts in fact according to the desire
for "recognition," but is not always aware of it (*ILH*, 498n =*IRH*,
226n).

In other words, there is no duty binding upon individuals and prior
to the concrete conditions of social existence. Morality cannot be kept
'pure' of social considerations because it is human, and man only
comes into being through struggle, an *inter*action with beings of his
kind.[37] In the beginning the potentially human *Homo sapiens* simply
wants to be recognized. Later, within human society, he expresses his
claim by saying that he *ought* to be recognized. As the process of
historical mediation continues, the 'he' that he seeks to have recognized
comes to include religious, political and moral principles—all of his
nonnatural desires. Human action in the entire developed society will
have two aspects. There will be 'struggle' by groups or individuals to
have their ideas and ideals recognized, if possible by everyone: the
'politics' of the society. And there will be 'work' to live according to
the ideas presently recognized: the 'mores' of the society. On the one
hand, others ought to recognize my human worth; on the other, I ought
to act so as to be recognized by them freely and *en pleine connaissance
de cause*. The first aspect of human action corresponds to mastery, the
second to slavery. And it is easy to see that the Christian and Kantian
teaching of conscientious submission to duty without regard to
consequences is simply the element of slavery in human action
abstracted from that of mastery.

Every real person is a synthesis of these elements, but in some
mastery predominates and in others slavery. Let us take for example an
athlete: he is a Master insofar as he desires to be recognized as victor
and a Slave insofar as he works to deserve such recognition. If the
Master gets the better of the Slave in him he may aim simply at the
external rewards of victory and forget about genuinely performing

---

[37]"Man does not merely risk his life: he also knows that he *ought* to do so.
And he is not content to work: he knows that work is a *duty*. But it makes no
sense to say that man struggles or works *because* that...is his duty. On the
contrary, he only has a notion of duty because he works and struggles. For it is
this struggle and work which create him qua human being *opposed* to natural
being. And the notion of *duty* is nothing but the manifestation of this
opposition" (*PD*, 248). In a word—anthropology before morality.

well—in other words, he may cheat. But even so, the slavish element is not absent: he would, presumably, prefer fair victory to unfair, if he were sure of being able to obtain it. People cheat because they fear defeat and prefer even unfair victory (unearned recognition) to it.

A perfectly slavish athlete, on the other hand, would work 'conscientiously' to become the best he could, but would have no interest in competing, or even in being observed. But, though cheaters abound, it is difficult to find a single example of an absolutely conscientious person. The Christian explanation for this would be that man, having fallen through pride, can never attain perfect humility. The Hegelian explanation would be that slavery always presupposes mastery. We begin not in any state of prideless perfection but by desiring recognition of our importance. This remains a part of us in some form as long as we are alive and human. The desire to *earn* recognition and the creation of ideal recognizers are transformations of that original desire, cannot be found apart from it, and cannot be accounted for without reference to it.

Kant was aware of the oddity of pure conscientiousness and so asserted the need for 'completing' moral philosophy with the postulate of a kingdom of ends ruled by God, who in Kojèvian terms is an Ideal Recognizer. He has been much criticized by his commentators for this supposed inconsistency. But on the Hegelian view he was correct—human action, including 'moral' action in the Kantian sense, does imply the idea of recognition in some form. Kant's mistake, indeed, was to make it a mere appendage of moral thought rather than the very foundation of the moral life.

In sum: the element of slavery informs the primitive demand for recognition of one's human desires with a willingness to recognize those of others, that is, to change one's own desires (or ideals, or 'values'). In the first instance this is mere submission to the authority of another. But as a society develops and is mediated by further human action, this submission becomes a sense of duty to an ideal. Slavery is thus the source of much of what we call 'moral.' Moral action cannot be 'reduced' to a desire for recognition (or rewards, or consequences of any sort) any more than the Slave can be reduced to a 'kind' of Master. But neither can conscientious action be wholly divorced from such external considerations, any more than a Slave can exist without a Master.

L.   The Origin of Discourse

On the classical account, rational speech is our most important irreducible specific difference. The rejection of this teaching was one of Hobbes's most significant innovations. But he failed to provide any account of speech's supposed 'invention,' leaving his anthropology more obscure and less plausible as a rival to the classical than it might otherwise have been. Here again we shall find that Kojève's teaching is a fuller attempt than Hobbes's own to carry the Hobbesian or modern project to a conclusion.

Kojève certainly shared the view that discourse is not the primitive and irreducible human fact. In a summary discussion of dialectics, for example, he writes:

> One might be tempted to say that Being is only dialectical insofar as it is revealed by Thought [that is, rational thought or discourse], that it is Thought which gives Being its dialectical character. But this formulation would be incorrect or, at least, could lead to a misunderstanding. Because for Hegel it is rather the converse which is true: Being can only be revealed by Thought, there is only a Thought in and of Being, because Being is dialectical; which is to say—because Being involves a negative or negating constituent element [viz., human action]. It is the real dialectics of existing Being [= history] which is, among other things, the revelation of the Real and of Being by Discourse or Thought (*ILH*, 448-449 =*IRH*, 171).

Or, more succinctly: "Negation, Freedom and Action do not arise from thought, nor from self-consciousness, nor from external consciousness; it is rather these latter which arise from the Negativity realizing and 'revealing' itself (by thought in Consciousness) qua effective free action" (*ILH*, 495 =*IRH*, 223).

Since the struggle for recognition is the first action, all rational thought presupposes it. Can we find anything in the anthropogenic act which might mark it as the remote source of *logos*?

All human discourse is abstractive. Qualities are 'abstracted' or 'taken out' of things 'in thought' which are not *really* separable. So-called concrete objects are similarly abstracted from their 'given' place in the world (for example, I can speak of a tree without mentioning sunlight or water, though no tree can *really* exist apart from these). Things and qualities are given an autonomous, 'unnatural' discursive existence, in which they can be freely arranged and recombined (*ILH*, 542-543; *IDPH*, 126-127; greatly expanded upon in *CTD*, 111-147).

This freedom, which we all know to be characteristic of our thought, is intimately connected with human freedom as such. Prehegelian philosophy also, while it may never have been a 'philosophy of freedom' in Kojève's sense, usually asserted that only a rational or speaking being could be accountable for his actions. Hegelianism merely reverses the traditional formulation, by saying that only a free being could develop speech (*ILH*, 345-346n1 =*IRH*, 111n7).[38] Now, the first human abstraction from the here and now occurs in the original encounter, where the two consciousnesses 'lose themselves,' see themselves in one another. An animal simply *is* its natural being; humans can, in thought, stand outside of themselves, as it were, *consider* their given being objectively. Thus they are able to make plans for its active transformation.

Since the combatants fight over an idea of themselves one might want to say that they are already self-conscious, already capable of human thought and thus 'in principle' of speech. This would be the classical view of the matter. Kojève's response is not difficult to infer from what has been said already. Going into the struggle, *Homo sapiens* may have a 'faculty' of speech (perhaps genetically determined), but this is pure potentiality. Discourse, like human desire, precedes the struggle in time but has no reality apart from it. It is real only insofar as it effects something. The first *active* human abstraction from nature is the voluntary risk of life: "It is by the autonomous acceptance of death that [man] 'surpasses' or 'transcends' the given-being which he himself is, this 'surpassing' being precisely the thought which 'reveals' that being to itself and others, illuminating it from outside, as it were, and from an inexistent beyond" (*ILH*, 523 =*IRH*, 254-255).

But struggle is merely a necessary, not a sufficient, condition for the development of speech. This is because the combatant and Master wants to transcend nature immediately, all at once—to be lord of all he surveys without paying attention to the various characteristics of particular things. His primitive self-consciousness is accepted 'as is' by the Slave, and so remains unchanged and undifferentiated. If the Master were to speak we might imagine his external-consciousness to be like

---

[38]Kojève's doctrine of universals might be characterized as an 'active nominalism:' "When it is a question of purely natural, particular, real entities...the universalizing negation is only carried out in and by the thought (or Discourse) of Man, that is *outside* themselves. And that is why it can be said that the natural entity is, in itself, particular. It is not also universal...except by and for Man, who thinks it or speaks of it" (*ILH*, 510 =*IRH*, 239).

that of the naive sense certainty of *Phenomenology*, chapter one: 'here is this; now is that.' His self-understanding might sound like the Fichtean Ego positing itself: 'I am I.'[39]

But the Slave realizes his superiority to nature one natural object at a time. Work is always concerned with particulars. In the course of his work he learns to distinguish the various properties of things (as Hegel describes in his second chapter) and to find unities and laws underlying the flux of immediate sensation (chapter three). Abstracting these properties and laws from nature, he comes to speak of them. Actively negating natural properties, he posits others in their place. And to have a discursively formulable procedure for doing so is to have an art or technique. *Logos* and *techne* are inseparable.

This is very much in the spirit of Hobbes, for whom speech is also derivative of the inquiring of consequences, that is, of the effort to master nature through the discovery and control of efficient causes. But for Hobbes men are *naturally* workers. They require no masters; mastery is simply one of their inventions, consented to because of its expected favorable consequences. The Hobbesian order is Slave, then speech, then Master.

Kojève, more plausibly, goes from Master to Slave to speech. In the following too brief passage he indicates of the importance of the element of mastery for the Slave's development of speech. The Slave, he says, works out of fear:

> But *this* fear is different from that which he experienced at the time of the Struggle: the danger is no longer *immediate*; the Slave merely *knows* that the Master can kill him; he does not *see* this in the homicidal expression. In other words, the Slave who *works* for the Master represses his *instincts* as a function of an *idea*, of a *concept*.... Now, to be able to transform the natural given as a function of a *non*natural idea is to find oneself in possession of a *technique*. And an idea which engenders a technique is a *scientific* idea or concept. Finally, to possess scientific concepts is to be endowed with Understanding, *Verstand*, the faculty of *abstract* notions (*ILH*, 176 =*IRH*, 48-49; see also *HMC* 354-355 =Eng. 33).[40]

---

[39]This, of course, is only true 'at the limit,' in the Master as an 'ideal type.'

[40]Kojève's thesis that thought is an aspect of work must on no account be confused with the well-known pseudohegelian teaching according to which thought is an effect of the *products* of work, or, as it is usually phrased, of 'material conditions.' The artifacts and institutions which constitute civilized man's material conditions are on the Hegelian view 'totalities,' formed from natural materials and human action. Action in turn is behavior informed by

The world is not first understood and then mastered; it is understood *as* it is being mastered, *insofar* as it is mastered. The discourse which reflects the world is an aspect of human labor upon it: knowing is making. And as with external-consciousness, so with self-consciousness. Since man *is* essentially his action, he must act before he has any 'self' to speak about or know. As the Slave works, his self-consciousness evolves through a series of ideologies which Hegel describes in chapter IV, B. In sum, it is only by bringing forth a human world that man can know either himself or the world around him. As Kojève puts it: "without creation by the action which negates, there is no contemplation of the given. [Hegel's] anthropology is fundamentally different from the Greek, for which man knows and recognizes himself first and then acts" (*ILH*, 49 bottom).

Indeed. On the classical view the arts presuppose *logos*. Architecture, for example, presupposes that the architect knows what a house *is*, that is, that he grasps the idea of a house, which does not vary throughout space and time. His art is the capacity to incarnate this preexisting idea in natural materials. To invent something is merely to be the first to perceive or realize the idea of it—or perhaps only the first since the last natural cataclysm. Man is thus not 'creative' in any strong sense.[41]

Classical thought involves no assumption that passive contemplation of the world or ideas preceded the arts *historically*. But it would tend to make of the historical priority of *technai* a mere accident of circumstance: in order to have leisure to contemplate, philosophers in fact need a regular supply of food, a tolerable amount of personal security, etc. For Kojève on the other hand, only work *creates* the concepts which inform objects and allow them to be contemplated. Human action is what *gives* the 'given.' Action is *essentially* prior to knowledge. Prior to action is only the chaos of

---

thought (animal behavior being purely natural). Following the doctrine of 'thought from material conditions,' we should have to reduce the discursive, human element in any given set of conditions to conditions still earlier—until we arrive at the state of nature. So this teaching implies that the human world is a special case of the natural world. That is why its devotees, however much they may like to throw the word 'dialectics' around, are usually explicit determinists.

[41]*Republic*, 596b: "Aren't we also accustomed to say that it is in looking to the *idea* of each implement that one craftsman makes the couches and another the chairs we use, and similarly for the other things? For presumably none of the craftsmen fabricates the idea itself. How could he?"

Note also how this teaching accords with the prephilosophical myth that men were taught the arts by a divinity.

IV. THE PHILOSOPHY OF HISTORY

A. From Anthropology to History

According to our ordinary way of thinking, anthropology should be the science of man and history the record of what man has done. But Hegelianism is, or at any rate includes, a historical anthropology: man *is* the product of all which he has *done*. Acting is certainly distinct from its product, just as—to take a hackneyed example—sculpting is distinct from sculptures. But just as obviously they cannot really be separated. Similarly, for the Hegelian, anthropology and the philosophical study of history are distinct but inseparable enterprises.

A fully articulated science of the human things would contain three parts. First, an account of what man is, always and everywhere. This does not, to say it once more, mean a description of any actual, natural traits peculiar to his species; it means an explanation of man's 'unnatural potentiality' (second-order desire), of the fundamental kinds of action arising from it (work and struggle), and of some of the concepts implied by such desire and action (for example, freedom, recognition, planning and mediation).[1] This is Hegelian 'anthropology' in the strict sense. The second part would be an explanation of historical events and epochs as mediated forms of the same human desire and action described in the first part. This is the philosophy of history. And the third part would be a systematic description of the human world produced by the actions of history: politics, law, religion, mores, art, philosophy and so on.

In the last chapter we outlined Kojève's version of Hegelian anthropology: his 'timeless' and therefore abstract description of man. Now we must see how he sets that anthropology in motion and provides it with a concrete content in an interpretation of the

---

[1]"There is something in Man, in *every* man, which renders him fit to participate—passively or actively—in the realization of universal history" (*ILH*, 162 =*IRH*, 32 bottom).

philosophy of history presented by Hegel in chapter six of the
Phenomenology.

The general principles underlying Kojève's Hegelian philosophy
of history are identical with those of the struggle for recognition; they
involve the same understanding of nature, freedom and truth.[2] We can
illustrate this by briefly considering the French Revolution, which
Kojève often treats as paradigmatic.

When people pass judgment upon an institution such as the French
Monarchy or upon the acts which overthrew it, they ordinarily feel—
indeed, they must feel—that there is some basis in reality for their
convictions. But the overwhelming majority of men have neither the
time nor the inclination to inquire carefully into what that basis might
be. Those who do so are called 'philosophers.' Among them, it is
perhaps those in the classical tradition whose views are most similar to
those of nonphilosophers. Reflecting its origin in Socratic conversation,
classical thought takes seriously the possibility that the 'naive' man, in
so confidently pronouncing judgment, does perceive something real
about the world: underneath the flux of human affairs there exist
naturally authoritative and unchanging principles. The rigorous analysis
and refinement of our original or unreflective views allows us partially
to grasp them. The evaluation of a French Revolution depends upon the
idea of natural right at which one has arrived. The perennial
embarrassment of classical philosophy is, of course, that no two
philosophers ever seem to arrive at precisely the same idea.

Hobbes rejects natural right, but shares with the classical tradition
the belief that there is a *preexisting* standard for judging of regimes and
revolutions. This standard is the convention or compact underlying all
commonwealths. The essence of the Hegelian teaching, on the other
hand, is that *the only standards for the evaluation of historical events
are produced by history itself.* Outcomes, not origins, are authoritative.

For example, the prerevolutionary *philosophes* or intellectuals
rejected the state in which they lived in the name of an idea, or rather a
set of somewhat nebulous ideas. These ideas had no 'basis' whatsoever;
they were merely a form of human desire, pure possibility, nonbeing.
But the *philosophes*, like the combatants in the original struggle,
identified themselves with their human desires and ignored as much as
possible their 'given' being within a Catholic monarchy. This gave

---

[2]"This dialectic [of Master and Slave] does not concern individual
relations only. But equally: Rome and the Barbarians, the Nobility and the
Third Estate, etc." (*ILH*, 53).

them, like the combatants in the anthropogenic struggle, a false view of themselves.

> All revolutionary action is self-negating. But the Revolutionary does not want to commit suicide, even if he wants to be considered an assassin.... He places himself (fancies he places himself) outside the Society (so as not to be involved in its downfall)—and for this reason he slanders Society.... [But] to denounce the Society is in fact to adhere to it. So the Revolutionary is a liar (*ILH*, 136).

Thus far Kojève's historicism appears (like Hobbes's teaching, superficially understood) to have 'conservative' implications. Not for long: "[The Revolutionary] is one with the Society qua its slanderer; in and by him the Society slanders itself: it itself is a lie and even—a conscious lie. The Slander is the sign of the weakness of the existing Society, not of the revolutionary Propaganda" (*ILH*, 136-137). How do we know this? Because we happen to be living after the Revolution and see that the Propaganda did, in fact, destroy the old Society. But the statement regarding relative strength refers to the situation before the Revolution. Was it already true *then* that the Propaganda was stronger, and merely unknowable because of the complexity of the situation? Perhaps—but in that case the Revolution was not a genuine struggle. What appeared to be free action was in fact a natural or quasi-natural unfolding of something predetermined, making explicit what had been true but implicit. In Kojève's words, if the Revolution is "a function of a *given* goal," then it is "*dependent* on the given World and not revolutionary" (ILH, 144). This would be the view of naturalism—and also, one could argue, of classical philosophy.[3]

On the Hegelian view there was no truth to the matter before the Revolution. The king might have had the Propagandists hanged. Perhaps this would have averted the revolution; certainly it would have forced it into a different form. Because all the actors of the Revolution had human or nonnatural desires, they were free. But once they had acted, the matter was settled. The action created a reality for our statements to correspond to, and we may *now* say that revolutionary propaganda was, in fact, stronger than prerevolutionary society simply because it did, in fact, destroy it.

In short, on the naturalistic and classical view, doing follows being; on the Hegelian view, being follows doing.

---

[3]Because classical philosophy cannot account for freedom: see above, Chapter III, Section G.

Once the Revolution has been carried out, the propagandists' slander is 'subsumed,' that is, destroyed qua slander but preserved under a new form:

> For to "slander" the new Society [in the same terms] is to say [or imply] that it does not differ from the old one. Now, this is *true* (in part), since the present implies the past.... The supposed Slander would then merely speak the truth. So it would be without *force* [for further change], for the truth reveals what *is* and does not *negate* anything. The "Slander" would not be a piece of propaganda at all, but a contribution to the better understanding of the new Society, that is, its affirmation, its reinforcement (*ILH*, 137 top).[4]

In plain language this means that once all the aristocrats have been killed, repeating the revolutionary propaganda in the past tense—'the aristocrats were bloodsuckers of the people'—will serve to justify the new order. One grasps that this doctrine is a kind of framework which could be given any content by events. It serves to justify success as such, or rather makes success self-justifying. Hobbes's equation of the right of sovereignty with the fact—with its consequence that all successful rebellions are legitimate—was the key precedent for this unpleasant aspect of Hegelian historicism.

B.   The Question of Historiographical Accuracy

We intend to give an account of the specific content of Hegelian historicism as presented by Kojève in his *Introduction to the Reading of Hegel*. But it will not be our concern to assess the accuracy of Hegel's or Kojève's historical identifications or interpretations. Any of these might be challenged in various ways without calling into question historicism itself or even Hegel's overall philosophy of history.

For example, chapter seven of the *Phenomenology* contains a section on Egyptian art and religion. Now, Hegel believed that the Greek *polis* was the first truly human political arrangement. This means that the prehellenic world was still 'natural;' the Egyptians could not have had (*in acto*) the human traits which presuppose the struggle for recognition. One of these is the negation of nature which we call 'work.' Therefore the Egyptians who built the pyramids could not

---

[4]Kojève remarks (*ILH*, 402n) that slander often does survive social change; successful revolutionaries still enjoy thinking of themselves as 'nonconformists.'

really have been working. And Hegel does not flinch from this strange conclusion; he calls the Egyptians' behavior "an instinctive working, like the building of honeycombs by bees" (*PG*, ¶691). He may have been led to this view by the relative uniformity of style and content in Egyptian art over a period of more than two millennia, as contrasted with the succession of styles and movements characteristic of later western art. But surely this relative uniformity cannot seriously be compared with the natural fixity of form in honeycombs or spiderwebs produced by animals of the same genetic makeup. Moreover, a natural uniformity should extend across space as well as time, and Hegel knew that the art and religion of other prehellenic peoples differed significantly from the Egyptian.[5]

We might leave it at this if our purpose were merely to turn the philosopher's gaffes to ridicule, after the manner of Bertrand Russell. But a more important matter is whether a better understanding of prehellenic civilization is possible on the basis of Hegelian anthropology. In other words, are Hegel's questionable interpretations of particular epochs essential to his historical anthropology? And it seems clear that they are not. In the present case, for example, we need merely shift the emergence of actualized humanity a good deal further back. For there may well have been a stage in human evolution to which Hegel's bee comparison correctly applies. According to the paleontologists there is a fairly direct correlation between the stages in the natural evolution of hominids and the kinds of stone tools and weapons they made. But this natural correlation ends with the emergence of biologically modern men (*Homo sapiens*). At that point *style* appears: artifacts from Europe and Africa and Asia no longer resemble one another. The rise of Egyptian civilization belongs to an epoch many thousands of years later; the Egyptians were no 'natural men.'

Analogously, Hegel's understanding of Greek civilization may indeed—as is so often said—have been overly influenced by Winckelmann and the Romantics, but still accurately reflect elements of our humanity originally created through free historical action. We shall not pursue such questions; our concern is the content given

---

[5]Kojève proposes an imaginative explanation for this 'natural diversity:' the various natural religions correspond to human desires not yet acted on. Animal sacrifice, for example, expresses *Homo sapiens'* potential for becoming a Master, pyramid building that for becoming a Slave (*ILH*, 239-241). This implies a 'realist' understanding of potentiality and thus contradicts historicism, a mistake he accuses Hegel of sometimes making: see *ILH*, 40.

historicist anthropology by the Hegelian philosophy of history as interpreted by Kojève.

C.   The Historical Realization of Mastery: the Greek *Polis*

Reading Hegel's comparison of one-sided with mutual recognition we may easily get the impression that the transition from one to the other, that is, history, is a straightforward matter: the Slave must negate the Master and the (former) Master must negate nature, that is, work. And we are all familiar with a 'philosophy of history' which follows this model precisely. According to it, history falls into two periods. In the first, extending to the present, the masses of enslaved humanity toil to support an idle and belligerent coterie of masters. In the second, scheduled to begin in the near future, the slaves rise up, wreak vengeance upon their oppressors, and inaugurate an endless age of justice and brotherhood. Hegel actually discusses this 'philosophy of history' in an entertaining chapter of the *Phenomenology* called "The Law of the Heart and the Frenzy of Self-Conceit." But it is manifestly *not* his own.

Kojève sometimes exposes himself to the charge of peddling a vulgar 'radicalism' as the Hegelian philosophy of history. He often speaks of history ending by the Slave resuming the struggle and putting the Master to death (*ILH,* 178, 496n, 502 =*IRH,* 50, 225n, 231; *PD,* 242). But this is a kind of shorthand or rhetorical flourish; in his more extended discussions it is clear he does not intend any such clumsy, literal application of the Master-Slave story. Instead of all human history being a 'history of class struggles,' it is a process whereby first mastery and then slavery "reveals its essence in realizing by Action its existential possibilities" (*ILH,* 173 =*IRH,* 45 top).

At the very outset we are faced with a difficulty. We saw above why mastery is unviable: the Master only actualizes his potential humanity by ceasing to exist. "One can only *die* as a Master (in a struggle for recognition), but one cannot *live* mastery" (*PD,* 242; compare interpretation of tragedy *ILH,* 253-254). How, then, could mastery have 'revealed its essence' in the lives of whole nations over the course of several centuries? (*ILH,* 98-99; *HMC* 353n =Eng. 32n). And in truth, it was only able to do so by compromising on its fundamental principle. This is as good a time as any to point out that Master and Slave are 'ideal types,' figures meant to represent elements or Hegelian 'moments' of our humanity: they are never found in a pure form. A perfect Master would fight with everyone he met until he had killed or enslaved the entire world. But it is evident that no man would, without assistance, be able to keep many others effectively enslaved—perhaps not even one (*OT*, 144). This means that anyone wishing to be a Master must grant *some* kind of recognition to *some* others without a struggle. Thus is formed a social class with common interests and purposes. Its members recognize one another (1) as slave holders, united in maintaining their mastery, and (2) as comrades-in-arms, united in battles with outsiders.

And there is another matter. However effectively a group of Masters keeps its Slaves in their place, however successful it is in wars with other Masters, it will still perish if it does not continuously reproduce itself. And reproduction is, as the reader is perhaps aware, a natural process. But mastery as such is a kind of superiority to and negation of animal nature. So it is not *qua* Master that the Master reproduces himself. Real Masters, unlike the ideal type in Hegel's story, have families. Their wives are not expected to struggle for recognition, yet they belong in some sense to the same social class: they are 'Masters by courtesy.' And the Masters' children must be humanized by education in the ideal of mastery.

In sum, the Master is most truly Master when fighting enemies and ruling Slaves, but he must also live as a citizen and head of family. These four statuses determine for Kojève the character of the ancient Greek *polis*, the historical realization of mastery.

One can discern a pattern among them. Citizenship is an impure version of, that is, a compromise with, the status of combatant: citizens are originally and fundamentally comrades-in-arms. And rule over one's family is an impure version of rule over Slaves: for family life is essentially directed toward the preservation and reproduction of the *natural* being of the Master just as the Slave's work is directed at the immediate satisfaction of the Master's first-order or nonhuman desires. According to Kojève, the first two statuses represent the universal element in the Master's humanity and in the *polis*, while the second two represent the particular element.

The Master's statuses may be represented in a table as follows:

	pure form:	impure form:
struggle with equals:	warrior	citizen
rule over inferiors:	slave holder	head of family

D. Its Difficulties

Mastery as such is impersonal. The risk of life which defines it is identical in all. When Masters band together and become citizens this universality or impersonality is transformed, but by no means disappears: it becomes equality under the law. The *polis* recognizes its citizens insofar as they are prepared to fight for it, that is, recognizes them as warriors and therefore in the manner of warriors—universally:

> The citizen of this State...is *an* anonymous warrior, not Mr. *So-and-so.* And even the Head of State is only an ordinary representative of the State.... In his activity he is a function of the State; it is not the State which is a function of his personal, particular will. In short, the Head of the Greek City-State is not a "dictator" in the modern, Christian, romantic sense of the term (*ILH*, 185 =*IRH*, 59).[6]

Slavery on the other hand differentiates, particularizes:

> The human value constituted by *Work* is essentially *particular,* "personal." *Bildung,* the educating formation of the Worker by Work, depends on the concrete conditions in which the work is carried out, which vary in space and are modified in time as a function of that work itself. So it is ultimately by Work that the differences between men are constituted, that "particularities," "personalities," are formed (*ILH*, 186 =*IRH*, 59).

Family life shares with slavery a concern with particulars: the head of the household is not an anonymous warrior to his wife and children. They love him—which, according to Kojève, means that they attach value to his *being*; this is to be distinguished from recognizing him, which would be to attach value to his *action*, that is, to admire something he has done. And because action is the essence of humanity, the quasi-recognition of familial love cannot humanly satisfy the Master. The family, indeed, continues to love its members in death, that is, when they no longer *are*; the cult of the dead is truly human. But this is merely another version of the dilemma the Master faces in the struggle, viz., that actualized humanity and natural existence (life) exclude one another. In the *polis* as in the primal struggle, the Master cannot *be* satisfied.[7]

---

[6]Compare Rousseau, *Social Contract*, III, xvi-xvii and IV, vi.

[7]This is actually not quite what Kojève says. He writes: "Since Love does not depend on *acts*, on the *activity* of the beloved, it cannot be stopped even by

Although both are 'particularist,' rule over one's family is clearly not the same as rule over Slaves. For example, the Master is concerned with the education of his sons, the future Masters. He is not aware and certainly does not intend that work should 'educate' his Slaves, bringing forth ideals which will eventually triumph over his own. So, to repeat, the family represents an attenuation of the principle of mastery.

In chapter IV, A, Hegel described the Master as an 'ideal type,' that is, the pure form of mastery. In chapter VI, A, he turns to the historical realization of this type, and the impure—transformed and attenuated—forms of mastery occupy a more important place. Of course, the citizens of the Greek city-state really did go to war and hold Slaves, but Slaves and enemies were, so to speak, at the margins of civic life. The 'ethical world,' as Hegel terms that life, is marked especially by conflict between the impure universality of citizenship and the impure particularity of the family. It is this conflict, and not any direct struggle between Masters and Slaves, which ultimately destroys that world. In Kojève's words, "The People qua set of Citizens enters into conflict with itself qua set of Families" (*ILH*, 103).

The Master begins life submitted to the 'divine law' of the family: he is loved in his natural particularity. When he comes of age he 'leaves' the family to live under the human law of the city. He seeks universal recognition of his humanity; he must *act*. But the action characteristic of a city of Masters is war, which destroys natural particularity: a crime against the family, a violation of its divine law. And the family is right, because human desire can only be satisfied by the recognition of particularity; the glorier of chapter IV did not want to be an anonymous warrior but to have his individual worth recognized.

On the other hand, the citizen may act as a particular, seeking glory for himself or his family in civic life. But the city of Masters is universalist, informed by a general will. Private action negates, that is,

---

his *death*. By loving a man in his *inaction* one considers him *as if* he were dead" (*ILH*, 187 =*IRH*, 61 top). We remarked above that it is precisely a person's acts which can continue to be admired or recognized even centuries after his death. Thus there are still people who admire Caesar, but it has been a very long time since anyone has loved him. Families do continue to love members they have lost. But instead of attributing this to the members having been considered as if dead while alive, we would say rather that they are considered as if alive even when dead. Now, to consider something as if it were something else is human, 'unnatural.' So on our account the cult of the dead is more characteristically human than the 'natural' affection for parents or offspring; according to what Kojève says in this passage it would have to be the other way around. And this would make it difficult to explain why family life could not satisfy the Master.

corrupts, the principle of mastery itself and therewith the city founded upon it. The extreme of such corruption is tyranny, the subordination of the *res publica* to the particularity of the tyrant and his family. This, of course, is a crime against the city's 'human law.' And the city is right, because the tyrant's particularity cannot be recognized—freely and *en pleine connaissance de cause*—by other Masters (that is, as it may be *loved* by the tyrant's family).[8]

In other words, all action in the ethical world is criminal: the universal action of the city is a crime against the family, while particular action is a crime against the city itself. The Master is in a tragic impasse. This is the socially realized and thus transformed version of the impasse the 'pure' Master of chapter IV found himself in: the choice between death and the unsatisfying recognition of a Slave.

E. How Classical Philosophy Would Resolve Them

An apparent solution to the Master's dilemma is offered by Socrates in the *Republic*: the fusion of family and city. But what Socrates envisages is universal *love* for each particular citizen, as well as for the universal (the city) by each particular. In other words, he makes the city into a family, but not the converse. This provides no true recognition, since it is unmediated by action (sc.: action which negates, as opposed to mere cyclical activity). Human desire is to *earn* the desire of others, to be recognized *en pleine connaissance de cause*; this, as we said, is its 'slavish' aspect. The flaw in Socrates' proposal is that of the ancient *polis* itself: not taking account of the human value of work, the negation of nature (as distinguished from the fulfillment of natural purpose).

Indeed, it is possible to see the theory of natural teleology itself as a projection of the Master's situation, as—to speak Marxese—an 'ideological superstructure' whose 'material base' is a slaveholding society. Recall that a purpose is, on the Hegelian account, merely a free or unnatural potentiality; it only acquires reality insofar as it is actualized by the negation of nature in view of it, that is, by work. To

---

[8]In a still-vigorous 'ethical world' particularist political action will fail and be punished by death. Such punishment is a kind of universal recognition of the criminal's particularity—but, as always in the Master's world, the recognition which might have satisfied human desire is incompatible with human *life* (see *ILH*, 103).

assert a human 'purpose-in-itself,' an ideal which is already 'somehow' real, 'by nature,' without anyone *doing* anything, is an implicit failure by philosophy to recognize work.

This interpretation of classical teleology is reinforced by consideration of the utopian character of classical political thought (Aristotle's included): the best *polis* would be 'such as one would *pray* for.' It is a logical possibility which might come about by chance, 'in the natural course of things.' Other, less good *poleis* fit less favorable circumstances; but neither Plato nor Aristotle says anything about altering the circumstances so as to *make* a better city a real possibility.[9]

Of course, if Socrates' just city were realized the problem of inadequate recognition would, so to speak, take care of itself. For the action of realizing it would itself mediate the love Socrates describes, transforming it into genuine recognition. And on the Hegelian view this is roughly what has happened. History is the story of how a number of Socrates' proposals have been realized: rule by wisdom, abolition of conventional inequality of the sexes, 'fraternity' of citizens. The modern State may be understood as the 'revealed reality' of what in the *Republic* is still ideology.

F.   Self-Destruction of the Master's World

In any case, that State did not come into being by philosophers accidentally becoming kings. Instead, the Master's ethical world had to give way to another, in which slavery could 'reveal its essence.' And once again, it is difficult to see at the outset how this would even be possible.

In the struggle for recognition the combatants are already Masters—even without having Slaves—in the sense that they are acting according to the principle 'glory or death.' But slavery presupposes mastery in such a way that the real existence of Slaves without Masters would appear impossible. And as long as there are Masters, the State by definition belongs to them. How then can slavery 'realize its existential possibilities?' Certainly not by direct rebellion, for even if the Slaves succeeded they would thereby simply cease to be Slaves. And it is the realization of the Slave *as such* which is needed if both elements of

---

[9]We are under no illusion that Hegelianism's ability to 'explain' classical thought in Hegelian terms constitutes a refutation of that thought. If we offer no Aristotelian 'explanation' of Hegel, it is only because this would not further our present purpose of investigating the modern project.

man's 'unnatural potential' are to be actualized (*ILH*, 183-184 =*IRH*, 57).

The solution to this problem is given by Hegel in chapter VI, A, b & c. It falls into two parts, corresponding to the universal and particular aspects of the ethical world. We consider first the particular. In fact, we broadly hinted at this aspect of the process in our remarks on tyranny above: it is the gradual corruption of the general will by particular, familial wills. Kojève describes it in these words:

> The immediate agent of [the pagan world's] ruin is, strange to say, Woman. For it is the Woman who represents the familial principle, that is, the principle of *Particularity* which is hostile to Society as such and whose victory means the ruin of the State, of the Universal properly so called. On the one hand, the Woman acts on the *young* man who is not yet completely detached from the Family, who has not yet completely subordinated his Particularity to the Universality of the State. On the other hand, and precisely because the State is a *warrior* State, it is the *young* man—the young military hero—who must assume power there in the end. And once arrived in power, this young hero (=Alexander the Great) asserts his familial, still feminine particularity. He tends to transform the State into his *private* property, into a family patrimony, to make the *citizens* of the State his own *subjects* (*ILH*, 188 =*IRH*, 62).

Secondly, the integrity of the *polis* is undermined by its very universalism, that is, by the aspect which it recognizes, or with which it identifies itself. In other words, it is destroyed by warfare, even—or most especially—when it is the victor:

> The laws of war, of brute force, are such that the stronger State must gradually swallow up the weaker ones. And the *Victorious City* thus gradually transforms itself into an *Empire*—the Roman Empire. Now, the inhabitants of the mother-city, the Masters properly so called, are too few to defend the Empire. The Emperor must have recourse to mercenaries. At once, the citizens of the City are no longer *obliged* to make war. And gradually, after a certain time, they cease to do so (*ILH*, 188 =*IRH*, 62).

After ceasing to struggle, the former Masters begin to think like their Slaves:

> What is the Pagan Master going to do? He is going to lose interest in the State (the Universal)...to adopt the (particularist) ideas of the Slave: Stoicism, Scepticism, and finally Christianity; he will thus

disappear qua Master, not in a revolution (as a consequence of a negating action of the Slave), but by natural disintegration, like an animal. The passage from the Ancient to the Christian State has a revolutionary value but it is not a true Revolution. (*ILH*, 105)

We know from chapter IV why it is inherently impossible for the Master ever to be satisfied: even if he kills or enslaves the rest of the universe he does not achieve the human recognition he sought, that is, a recognition he himself could recognize as worthy of his own humanity. We may now add that, having no worlds left to conquer, he would by the very completeness of his success necessarily cease to be a Master, cease to risk his life for glory. Mastery, like fire, destroys itself by the very process which nourishes it. And this is pretty much what happened to Rome. The Hegelian philosophy of history adds little on this point to what the Roman historians themselves said.

The self-destruction of mastery by the carrying through of its own principle turns out to fit well with its internal corruption, its 'emasculation' described above. By ceasing to fight, the Masters "can no longer offer any resistance to the particularism of the Emperor, who 'suppresses' them qua *Citizens* and transforms them into particulars belonging to his *patrimony*, into 'private persons.' In short, the former citizens become *slaves* of the sovereign" (*ILH*, 188-189 =*IRH*, 63 top). And the emperor himself is no true Master, no representative of the universal, of the community as such. He is an accidental particular like his subjects, and so gives himself over to amusements, bodily pleasures and the like. The community is thereby dissolved. The Roman Empire is not a state in the proper sense, but a vast and random assemblage of particulars. With this 'universal' triumph of the particular, the Slave's hour has struck.

G.   The Triumph of the Slave: the Roman Empire

Of course, particularity and slavery are not the same thing; otherwise the Roman Empire would exhaust the Slave's existential possibilities and he would have no history of his own. What is especially characteristic of slavery is rather the synthesis of humanity with particularity. Animals—or even stones—are naturally particular, distinguished by occupying different positions in space and time however much they may be intrinsically or qualitatively similar. Masters are particular with regard to their bodies, but combine particularity with a specifically human or unnatural ideal—'glory' or 'self-certainty'— which is identical in all Masters, that is, universal. But in the Master universality and particularity exclude one another: he can actualize his universality only by dying, by destroying his natural particularity. The Slave on the other hand works, which means that he realizes a universal idea or ideal in a particular time and place. In making an ax, for example, he embodies an unnatural idea—the form or essence of an ax—in naturally particular materials. And in transforming his world he ultimately transforms himself and the generations of humanity to come. For his and their future work will take place under different conditions, viz., in a world containing axes and a teachable method for making them. Work is thus the basis of all education, and together work and education are the human *principium individuationis*; they produce a *human* particularity which has nothing to do with bodily particularity.

The great achievement of the Roman Empire was the elaboration of a private law centered on the idea of property:

> The fundamental notion of Roman legal thought, that of the "legal person," corresponds to the *stoical* conception of human existence as well as to the principle of familial particularism. Like the Family, Private Law attaches an absolute value to the *Being* of Man pure and simple, independently of his actions. And as in the stoical conception, the value attributed to the "person" does not depend on the concrete conditions of his existence: everywhere and always one is a "legal person," and all are so equally (*ILH*, 189-190 =*IRH*, 63-64).

Law is a human phenomenon; no animal can be subject to the law except in connection with humans, that is, qua property of some sort (*PD*, 28-32). Therefore in recognizing a private legal status of each person Roman law does recognize a *human* particularity. In what way, then, is the recognition afforded by private law still inadequate, still incapable of satisfying the Slave's human desire?

In the very same way that Stoicism is an inadequate grasp of the Slave's situation. Stoicism identifies thought as the essential in man. And the Stoic philosopher's thought is certainly human, independent of the naturally—or socially—'given,' that is, free. But Stoicism fails or neglects to see that what will be the 'given' next year depends in part on what men are thinking now. Action—in particular the Slave's work—is behavior informed by free, specifically human thought. And the Slave's thought—for example, his idea of an ax and method for making one—is simply an aspect of work, of his action; by itself it is mere potentiality. Stoicism therefore has an unreal, abstract character; a working animal cannot rest satisfied with it. "All discourse which remains discourse ends by *boring* Man" (*ILH*, 180 =*IRH*, 53 bottom).

Analogously, Roman law recognizes a legal status, a fixed, nonnatural or human aspect tacked on to each particular *Homo sapiens*. But it takes no account of action, which is the true content of the Slave's humanity. Therefore it does not fully recognize the Slave, nor can its merely abstract recognition satisfy him.

In sum: the *polis* recognizes universality, the glorying which is identical in each Master and actualized in the indeterminacy of death. The Roman Empire recognizes particularity, the human particularity in which each person finds himself, that is, his 'given' situation, internal and external, natural and social. But to be human is to act, to realize a universal thought *in* particular objects and circumstances, to synthesize universality and particularity. Accordingly, human desire can only be satisfied by a recognition of action as such, a recognition which is itself—like the humanity which is its object—a synthesis of universality and particularity. The formation of a state embodying such recognition is the task of the next great period of world history.

H.   The Historical Significance of Christianity

The Masters, having become Slaves of the emperor, abandon the ideal of mastery and accept the 'ideologies' of their Slaves: first Stoicism (which is boring), then Scepticism (in which one cannot live), and finally Christianity. In this last they become equals of the emperor himself—'in the sight of God.' The process culminates in the emperor's (Constantine's) own conversion: all are henceforward Slaves of God. This is an alienation of Spirit (that is, of humanity), a projection into the beyond of the political situation in the Empire. For the Christian God, like the emperor, is a *universal* Master—rather than, say, the 'God of Israel.' Yet his rule is over particulars, over each Christian soul, without the state serving as intermediary (*ILH*, 191-192 =*IRH*, 66).[10]

From the outset the Christian is more self-conscious than the pagan. We, the phenomenological observers, saw the conflict between

---

[10]It sometimes requires a considerable effort of the imagination for modern liberals to grasp that the 'private' character of belief and worship is not a necessary and timeless aspect of religion. Hence their indignation at attempts by the modern philosophers—Hobbes, Rousseau, Hegel himself—to reestablish even partially the ancient view ('civil religion'). Yet liberal tolerance is itself merely an extension of Christian particularism.

universality and particularity in the ancient world; the pagan did not see it, experiencing it as a tragic destiny which destroyed him (qua pagan Master). The Christian, by contrast, *himself* grasps the opposition between universality and particularity: this is what makes him an 'unhappy consciousness.' The pagan tried to *live* universality and exclude natural or slavish particularity. But the Christian grasps that what would give satisfaction could only be a synthesis of universality and particularity, that is, for the universal to inform and 'raise up' his flesh.

Christian self-consciousness is, however, alienated; it understands itself to be consciousness of an external reality. The universal is conceived not as the state, a human reality of which the believer is a part, but as God, a being separate from all that is human. And the synthesis is conceived not as the universal recognition of each particular citizen by a state itself the universal work of all particulars, but as the incarnation of the divine universal in one particular man.

This provides no practical solution for the believer: he cannot *become* Christ. But he has a duty to imitate Christ. This is the Christian Slave's work (his 'good works'). The Christian *serves* God, and for the very same reason the Slave serves his Master: fear of death (here become hope of eternal life). And he is recognized by God only insofar as he has made a conscious and 'conscientious' effort. "One is *born* a pagan; one *becomes* a Christian" (*ILH*, 121).

This is why, in spite of its unrevolutionary or even conservative intent, Christianity necessarily transforms the world. No teaching incorporating an ideal of self-transformation could, once universally accepted, avoid having social consequences—however 'particularist' the goals of that teaching. "The Christian *wants* [consciously] *to realize* himself [that is, his particularity]; *unconsciously* he realizes a World [a universal, a social or political reality]" (*ILH*, 121).

And Kojève goes on to say: "that is why he feels himself a stranger in this world." In other words, the Christian is alienated from the state. This is the real counterpart to alienation from God, the ideal universal, as described in chapter IV, B.[11] It replaces the tragic pagan *conflict* between universality and particularity. And it marks a progress over paganism. For that conflict was only 'resolved' by the death of the

---

[11]And that alienation is, in turn, an ideological expression of the Slave's situation: seeing in another the human dignity he wants for himself. Comparing this with our account of the Master's historical difficulties in Section D above, one sees why Kojève was correct to find in the story of Master and Slave the fundament of the entire Hegelian philosophy of history.

pagan Master himself, that is, it could not be resolved by and for the pagan. But the Christian can, and eventually does, overcome his alienation from the universal: in a sense, he himself becomes the Christ.

Hegel's concept of alienation solves the problem of how Slaves can continue to live and work in a world from which true Masters have disappeared: ruler or ruled, all are henceforward 'Slaves of God.' As was the case with mastery, slavery's realization involves a compromise with its own principle. Here that compromise is evident precisely in the continued existence of hereditary classes of rulers and ruled. Indeed, inasmuch as it asserted universal liberty, equality and fraternity to be *already* real—in the 'kingdom of heaven'—Christianity was usually hostile to efforts to realize its own ideals on earth; it was neither explicitly nor intentionally revolutionary. (In Christian terms, work and struggle to realize the Christian ideal amount to Pelagianism, a proud arrogation of what can and should only be effected by divine grace.)

Nevertheless, the Christian principle of universal equality before the divine Master informs even the most hierarchical political formations in Christendom, making them essentially different from the *polis*. For example, instead of identifying himself with his status as citizen and submitting his particularity to the general will of the city, the feudal lord views the state as "an *Other*." He "*serves* this Other to be paid, to be recognized." Even warfare is reinterpreted 'slavishly:' "The Lord, in making war, *works*. His job is war; dealing death, his trade." Couldn't one say the same about the pagan Master? No: the Master fights because he already *is* a Master—from the beginning, 'by nature' (according to his own self-understanding).[12] For the Christian Pseudo-Master it is the other way around. "It is not enough to be born and to *be*, to be a Feudal Lord. It is necessary to *act* (wage war) to *become* one" (*ILH*, 125).[13] The Christian warrior further attenuates the ancient ideal of mastery by his faith that God will save his soul from death.

The Commoner, on the other hand, is a Pseudo-Slave, one with no this-worldly Master. Lord and Commoner are called, with reference to

---

[12]Contrast Aristotle, *Politics*, I, 1255b13-15: the (legal) Slave who feels 'the opposite of affection' for his Master thereby reveals the preexistent, natural fact that he is not a Slave. Analogously, on these principles, warfare would reveal Masters but never make them.

[13]The Master as such only struggles for mastery or for independence, that is, to avoid being mastered by others; his motive is unmediated self-certainty. Wars of religion and other forms of 'ideological' struggle involve mediated forms of self-consciousness and belong to a later historical period (compare Rousseau, *Social Contract*, IV, viii). The Master would not be able to recognize the full human value of such struggle.

what they have in common, 'Bourgeois.' The history of the Christian world is the story of the gradual elimination of the pagan inheritance— the opposition between Lords and Commoners—and in the realization of bourgeois equality. Then, in the French Revolution and its aftermath, the opposition between the state and the individual is suppressed.[14]

I.   The Historical Significance of Speech

This process begins in language. That should not be surprising, for an elimination of opposition (overcoming of alienation) is a kind of action. And all action is the transformation of the 'given' in view of a plan, a discursive nonnatural potentiality. So that to understand, for example, what the French Revolutionaries *did*, one must have some understanding of what the intellectuals of the Enlightenment had *said* in the generation preceding.

But Hegel says something much more radical and surprising, viz., that only in the bourgeois Christian world does language "emerge in its characteristic significance" (*PG*, ¶508).[15] In other words, the French Revolution is not distinguished from political revolutions in the pagan world merely by the *kind* of talk current in its time, but also by talk itself having acquired a function it could not possibly have had in pre-Christian society. Here is why.

The characteristic significance Hegel refers to is the synthesizing of universality and particularity. All language emanates from particular beings; only in story books are there voices which whisper in the breeze. And all language has some outward form or embodiment— vibrations in the air, lines on paper—which is as particular as a natural object. But I may speak or write the *same* statement twice; plurality of utterance does nothing to diversify meaning.[16] And when I, a particular person, address others, my thought becomes the universal thought

---

[14]Compare *ILH*, 125 top and 128 bottom. That the Bourgeois is a Pseudo-Master *and* Pseudo-Slave does not contradict his function as the historical realization of slavery in particular. Lords and Commoners are both transformations of the original pagan Masters and Slaves—hence the 'pseudo'—but that which transforms them is the Christian idea of *slavery* to God.

[15]Kojève, commenting on this passage (*ILH*, 26), calls language a "specifically Christian phenomenon."

[16]Of course, the strict identity of meaning must be distinguished from the always relative similarity of outward form (or 'morpheme,' in Kojève's terminology).

(though not necessarily belief): everyone 'gets my meaning.' In other words, meaning is universal, unlimited in space and time.

Now, this synthesizing of universality and particularity—this incarnating of a universal thought in a particular utterance—belongs to language in all times and circumstances. But the political situation of the ancient world was such that language could not come into its own as a historical force. The tragic dilemma of the pagan Master—and of his social embodiment, the *polis*—is the mutual exclusion of universality and particularity. In that world "language has the Essence [that is, the universal, the *polis* as such] for its content and is the form of that content." It is "law and command," law being the verbal expression of citizenship, command that of rule over family and Slaves (*PG*, ¶508).[17] Hegel does not mention any particularist functions of language in the pagan world, but it obviously had them: for example, within the family (whenever the father was not merely commanding) and in the education of children. But the Master identifies himself with the universal; the particularism of family life represents a compromise with his ideal. So what will happen if language acquires a political function, that is, if it begins to synthesize universal and particular within the *polis*?

Well, we have already seen that the *polis* was corrupted when the young hero asserted his familial particularity in the public realm. One might well ask whether language did not have a hand in this process. The purest embodiments of mastery were the 'laconic' Spartans or Roman republicans of the type of Cato the Censor. It was the rising importance of rhetoric in Athens and the late Roman Republic which opened the way for demagoguery and the subversion of the Master's ideal.[18] In other words, the synthesizing character of language means that it cannot have a positive function qua language in the tragic world where universal and particular exclude one another.

The situation is quite the opposite in the Christian world of alienation. For to synthesize universality and particularity is precisely to overcome their alienation. In the end this must occur through action: that of the French Revolution. But action is behavior informed by discourse, and is preceded by discourse simply. Most of the rest of *Phenomenology*, VI, B, III, is therefore devoted to the *talk* of the *ancien régime*.

---

[17]The fourth status of the Pagan Master, that of warrior, is essentially silent.

[18]The influence of Rousseau on Hegel's view of the ancient world is everywhere unmistakable: on this point particularly that of the *First Discourse*.

J.	From Feudalism to French Absolutism

The first work of language is the transformation of feudalism into absolutism. This process has two sides: the private, still mostly particular consciousness of the Feudal Lord and the public, still mostly universal consciousness of State Power. Let us consider the former: "The Feudal Lord, as a landowner, represents the principle of Particularity, but he is one with the Universal by his military service. So in himself he is double; there is conflict between the private proprietor's interests and his duty as a warrior serving the State: for this reason he starts to *speak*; he clarifies and reveals the contradiction through Language" (*ILH*, 127).[19]

Across from the Feudal Lord, a particular consciousness with a universal ideal, there stands the State Power, a universal consciousness with a particular embodiment, viz., the king. And the king, too, begins to speak. He 'resolves,' in speech, the conflict between his particularity and the universality he incarnates: "I am the State." This speech is not an error, because it harmonizes with its object, the speech of the Feudal Lord (now become a Courtier).[20] The monarch, says Hegel, "knows himself, this particular, to be the universal power in that the nobles group themselves around the throne not only as prepared for the service of the State Power but also as an ornamental setting, and in that they are continually *telling* him who sits on it what he *is*" (*PG*, ¶511). In other words, absolutism marks a progress over feudalism in that the nobles no longer merely die silently for the state but also live and talk for it. But they do not act for it; all their action is directed to private ends (court intrigues, etc.). The king, for his part, inherits his power, that is, acquires it 'naturally.' He *sits* on his throne and *is* (king)—but does not *do* anything to earn his courtiers' praise (as Napoleon will).

---

[19]Recall Kojève's remark that "language is born of discontent."

[20]The reader may object that not the speech of the courtiers but the state itself was the object of Louis' celebrated remark (perhaps because the *word* state is its grammatical 'object'). This is to commit the error of reification; the state is not a thing separate from the thought and action of those who compose it.

In fact, Louis was expressing by this remark his human desire that all other human or nonnatural desires be assimilated to his own—in other words, that his humanity be universally recognized. And for this to happen, for his will truly to coincide with the (relatively) universal will of the kingdom of France, it was indeed necessary for his subjects to accept his authority. The flattery of his courtiers is the verbal expression of such acceptance or recognition. Therefore, in order for his self-assessment 'I am the state' to have truth, it must correspond to their own thoughts expressed (the king will want to presume) in their speech. So their speech, or the thought it represents, was the true object of his remark.

And finally, the 'ignoble consciousness'—the Third Estate—is simply ignored, that is, left unrecognized. "So Versailles is not a *Wirklichkeit* [an actuality]; it is still an 'Ideal,' a 'project'—which the Revolution will later realize" (*ILH*, 128).

The spirit of State Power *as such*, that is, when it is as it ought to be, is to have its own actuality and nourishment in the action of its citizens as well as in their thought or speech. But now State Power is an empty name. What we might call the 'effective Power of the State,' the action of its members, is given over to private ends. There is contradiction between word and deed; State Power is alienated. The universal is a mere 'moment of self-consciousness,' something for particulars to exploit. Now, the conventional or socially recognized power of the human particular qua particular is just what we ordinarily call money or property. So at this stage the king is transformed into a mere dispenser of wealth, and wealth becomes 'king.' The Christian State, says Kojève, "comes to depend on Property, Wealth, Capital, that is, on what for the Christian is Evil" (*ILH*, 128).

The wealthy and refined aristocrat of eighteenth-century France, one perceives, no longer bears much resemblance to the Feudal Lord—not to speak of the Pagan Master. On the other hand, he is beginning to look suspiciously like the ignoble consciousness who "sees in the sovereign power a fetter and a suppression of being-for-itself and therefore hates the ruler, obeys only with concealed malice, and is always on the point of rebellion" (PG, ¶501). This should not surprise us; the homogenizing of Noble and Commoner, their transformation into the Bourgeois, is simply the practical rejection of pagan mastery (as the adoption of Christianity was its rejection 'in principle').

Wealth has now usurped the function of State Power. And the second aspect according to which Hegel had distinguished noble from ignoble consciousness was precisely its attitude toward wealth. The ignoble consciousness "sees in it, through which it attains to the enjoyment of being-for-self, only the disparity with the lasting *Essence* [that is, roughly, society], since through wealth it comes only to consciousness of particularity and transitory enjoyment" (PG, ¶501). Now, as we might have predicted, the noble attitude to wealth begins to merge with the ignoble one:

Wealth has become a *Gegenstand* (an external, objective reality) to whose laws the Bourgeois is subjected as the Pagan is to those of the State (and the Idle Man to those of Nature). But Wealth is in fact the Bourgeois' *product*, created by him to oppose the Universal of the State. However, the Bourgeois thereby alienates himself and is

subjected to the yoke of his exclusive Particularism just as the Master
was subjected to the yoke of his unilateral Universalism (*ILH*, 129).

K.   The Enlightenment as a Social Movement

We have arrived at the extreme point of the Slave's social
embodiment. The last remnant of pagan mastery is a foppish *bon
vivant*; the universal laws of the state have been largely replaced by the
'universal laws of wealth,' that is, 'laws' of something created by
particulars for particulars. The Bourgeois is a Slave to himself, his
alienated self.

The original Slave ideology, we recall, was Stoicism: a disregard
for the external world, understood as purely accidental circumstance.
This was an attitude appropriate to an early stage of slavery's historical
realization, when the inherited forms of the Master's world retained
much of their original vigor. For then the external world did not, in
fact, have much to do with the Slave's own humanity; it *was*
'accidental' as far as he was concerned.[21] But the eighteenth-century
Bourgeois lived in a world formed and informed by the Slave's work.
He was living in a house he had built, so that to disregard his
circumstances would have meant disregarding himself. Instead, says
Hegel, this self-consciousness

> sees...its 'I' outside itself and belonging to another, sees its
> personality as such dependent on the accidental personality of
> another, on the accident of a moment, a caprice, or some other utterly
> indifferent circumstance.... Everything that has continuity and
> universality, that is called law, good and right has fallen apart and
> perished.... The pure 'I' itself is absolutely disrupted (PG, ¶517;
> compare ¶194).

Even being rich is no solution to the problem, because of the
accidental and impersonal character of wealth; the rich Bourgeois, as
Kojève says, possesses only particular wealth and not Wealth itself ("*il
ne possède que* des *richesses, et non* la *Richesse*") (*ILH*, 130).

---

[21]This was only strictly true in the state of nature, that is, at the point
where humanity as such first emerged. Obviously someone was building
houses and baking bread in the *polis*, and it was not the Master qua Master. But
it is perhaps appropriate that the first well-articulated form of slavish thought
reflects the original or 'natural' condition of the Slave.

We saw that the verbal manifestation of absolutism was the king's identification of himself with the universal (the state), as well as the reflection of that identification in the flattery of his courtiers. Now a new sort of speech arises to make manifest the Spirit of the world of wealth—the speech of Rameau's Nephew, "absolutely frank and sincere, who reveals what he is, that is, a lie" (*ILH*, 131). With obvious relish he explains how he flatters the foolish *amour propre* of the wealthy in order to sponge off them, all the while laughing behind their backs. And across from him—his courtier, so to speak—sits an 'honest consciousness,' the *moi* of Diderot's dialogue. He is scandalized by the overt hypocrisy and snobbish servility of the younger Rameau, but all his attempts at refutation merely reflect and confirm Rameau's words. For example, if the honest man points to something admirable in the world of wealth, he is shown how it is dependent upon what is base and cannot be separated from it in fact. Or if he asserts the possibility of withdrawing from the 'perverted world' he is shown how the withdrawal itself is conditioned by the world and its perversion.[22] This 'language of turbulence' is now the middle term that mediates man with the world of wealth, his alienated Self.[23]

The 'bourgeois intellectual,' of whom the younger Rameau is an example, "has already got beyond the Bourgeois World in and by his speech" (*ILH*, 131). How so? According to Hegelian anthropology all men have got beyond the natural world in and by their action, that is, behavior mediated by unnatural or human thought. Such thought can indeed be *im*mediately expressed in speech, but is realized only in the products of human action.[24] In other words, speech alone never demonstrates *actual* superiority.

In the present case we are dealing not with man as such and the natural world, but rather with a certain kind of man and a certain spiritualized or humanized world. How can we know the intellectual is better than this world, as Kojève asserts? Certainly not simply because

---

[22]Just as eremitism, for example, was a product of Christian *society* rather than a return to the state of nature. The younger Rameau's point is genuinely Hegelian.

[23]This perhaps sounds like the perfect example of an arbitrary 'metaphysical' interpretation foisted onto the historical record, but compare Burke's observation (in *Reflections on the Revolution in France*) that the 'philosophical cabal' "served as a link to unite...obnoxious wealth to restless and desperate poverty."

[24]Speech "is the outward-existence (*Dasein*) of the pure self qua self [that is, what we have been calling 'humanity' or 'man qua man'].... Otherwise the 'I' as this pure 'I' is not there. In every other expression it is immersed in an actuality and is in a form from which it can withdraw itself" *PG*, ¶508.

he is able to mock at it; his wealthy patrons are 'speaking animals' too, and therefore potential mockers. We may grant that nowhere on earth is a greater 'subjective certainty' of personal superiority found than in the mind of an intellectual, but introspective evidence is not admissible in a Hegelian court (*OT*, 153-155). Again the difficulty confronts us of finding an objective criterion for wisdom as long as men "see their own wit at hand and other men's at a distance."

This difficulty, according to the Hegelian teaching, has no *discursive* solution. It can only be resolved through human action. But the intellectual is essentially a talker.

> He reduces himself to the "Speaking Consciousness"—and the World, like the "Honest Man," listens to him without getting too excited. The result is *Eitelkeit*, the vanity of everything. You remark upon it—and go about your business. "Rameau's Nephew" is thus a clearly conformist attitude, in spite of its nihilistic and sceptical appearance (*ILH*, 131).

Inaction is in fact the defining principle of the intellectual for Kojève.[25] And we do observe that large numbers of 'critical thinkers' are able to find much self-contentment in this sort of talk. But it cannot *satisfy* the desire of an essentially working and struggling animal.

So, like the Stoic who becomes bored with his private thoughts, the intellectual tires of coffeehouse chatter. But he cannot pass directly to action. Under the *ancien régime* he had little possibility of advancement because the state was a hereditary aristocracy (a *Sein* rather than a *Tun*). And in any case, to advance within the 'perverted world' would contaminate the purity of his principles. But there is a way around this. "The actions of men proceed from their opinions, and in the well-governing of opinions consisteth the well-governing of men's actions."[26] How does one govern opinions? Sometimes by direct

---

[25] A favorite theme of Kojève's. See, for example, *ILH*, 89, commenting on 'Virtue and the Way of the World': "The Virtuous Man places all value in the particular as he is in his struggle against the *Weltlauf*; consequently, he must preserve himself qua 'struggler,' consequently, he does not, at bottom, want to change the given society." This is the gist of the Hegelian critique of Kantian ethics, viz., the notion that one's will can be good apart from all considerations of consequences.

[26] *L*, xviii. The passage continues: "in order to their peace and concord." For Hobbes well-governed actions are above all peaceable; therefore good government essentially involves the propagation of 'peaceable opinions.' So far truth is not a concern. But then he adds: "doctrine repugnant to peace can [not] be true." In other words he asserts a natural harmony between truth and the most important end of political association. This is *the* defining principle of

action, such as the censoring of books. But also merely by talk of a certain kind, viz., the spreading of unfamiliar ideas—propaganda. In other words, since a state is a union of speaking animals, to *speak* to them can itself be, indirectly, to act upon the state. "If *everyone* speaks like Rameau's Nephew the World by that very fact will be changed. Rameau's Nephew *universalized*—that is the *Aufklärung* " (*ILH*, 135).

The initial result of enlightenment is that bourgeois society ceases to believe in itself. It entangles itself in a contradiction, continuing to affirm by its action what it negates in its thought and speech. In the long run no society can continue to exist in this manner. And so the "coffeehouse revolution" did indeed prepare the way for the real one.

L.   The Thought of the Age of Enlightenment

In fact, nothing remains to be *done* now but call the Estates General. But before moving on to the Revolution, we must consider the content of bourgeois or Christian thought. We are not concerned with the existential attitude of the Christian as such, that is, the 'timeless' individual Christian Hegel described as the Unhappy Consciousness. Nor with theology, treated in chapter seven of the *Phenomenology*. Instead, we are now concerned with a social and historical phenomenon—the self-consciousness of Christendom.

It is characteristic of the Christian world of alienation for thought to appear in a dual form, as two antagonistic doctrines or tendencies. On the Hegelian view their opposition is superficial: each reflects an isolated aspect of the Christian world and is false only insofar as it takes itself to reflect the whole. After the active suppression of alienation in the Revolution, both will be integrated in a single, comprehensive system of thought—which is, of course, Hegel's own.

In the *Phenomenology* Hegel presents three such pairs of mutually hostile doctrines. The first consists of Faith and Pure Insight. Faith is pretty much Christianity as ordinarily understood. We have seen

---

the enlightenment; it should be understood by way of contrast with the characteristically classical teaching of the 'noble lie.'

Hobbes hoped "this writing of mine may fall into the hands of a sovereign," that is, that he would be able to enlighten a despot. The propagandists Hegel had principally in view were enlightening 'from below.' This, apart from the truth or even content of their doctrine, goes some way toward explaining the degree of peace and concord Frenchmen came to enjoy once they had acted upon their instructions. One can only admire the adaptability of the modern project.

already that it is essentially a projection of the Slave's situation—God being, for example, an idealized Master embodying the Slave's alienated humanity. Pure Insight is roughly Cartesian rationalism; Kojève identifies it also with the Reason of *Phenomenology*, chapter V. Its essential character is critical or negative, reflecting the work of the Slave. Like work, it requires material; it cannot subsist independently. Predictably, it finds its principle material in Faith. Hence it appears to be the anti-Christian form of thought *par excellence*. But the object of Christian Faith is an eternally self-identical Being, unalterable by human action and incomprehensible by human thought—in other words, a Being like the unchanging Pagan Master, a Being not specifically Christian. So in spite of appearances it is the critical spirit of Pure Insight which expresses what is properly Christian in Christian thought, viz., negativity as opposed to 'given-being.'[27]

When it gets to the end of its criticism of Faith, Pure Insight is left with nothing; it is incapable of genuinely overcoming (subsuming) the content to which it was opposed. Instead it 'posits' an incomprehensible Other (similar in this to the ancient sceptic who became an Unhappy Consciousness). In other words, it returns to Faith—which then, in principle, would call forth a new critical effort on the part of Pure Insight. "Faith and Christian Reason mutually engender and destroy one another" (*ILH*, 133). They are analogous to the paradox: 'the following statement is true; the foregoing statement is false.' There seems to be a sort of motion, but it does not lead anywhere.

In the end, that is, in the French Revolution, work and struggle, the active counterparts of Pure Insight, will realize the Christian ideal (Faith). So we, the phenomenological observers, may say that the two opponents were unconsciously working toward a single result. Then, and only then, they can both take their place in the single system of thought which accurately reflects that result.

Before that happens there is an ideal or 'ideological' development within Christian thought itself. Faith and Pure Insight evolve into Deism and Sensualism, respectively. And these evolve, finally, into Idealism and Materialism. The specific contents of these forms of thought are less important than the overall tendency and result of the process of which they are Hegelian moments. Christian Faith has been emptied of all content. The restless spirit of critical rationalism has

---

[27]Contrast Descartes' point of departure in the *Meditations* with Aristotle's statement that philosophy begins in wonder.

become a belief in colorless, odorless, inert matter—a 'given-being' of a sort which does not improve upon the Lord of Hosts:

> 'Pure Matter' can no more account for the wealth of Nature than 'Pure Spirit' for the wealth of History. The two parties of the *Aufklärung* have not succeeded in getting beyond Cartesian metaphysics so as to understand that intrinsically Being and Thought are identical. To tell the truth, they *are* not identical: they merely *become* so in the course of History. It is by *Action* that Thought comes to be (real) and that Being is thought. (*ILH*, 140)

Idealism and Materialism have in common the denial of transcendence. In other words, neither is alienated. We may say that the alienation or transcendence present in earlier bourgeois forms of thought taken separately has now been reduced to the opposition *between* these last two. And that helps to explain why they appear so paltry when compared to the more complex forms of thought from which they arose. A static, undifferentiated spirit is just the thing to hover over the face of static, undifferentiated matter.

Among the most important things to disappear with the suppression of alienation (in thought) is the notion of *service*: of the Master by the Slave and of God by the Christian. In the increasingly homogeneous bourgeois world it is no longer clear for whose or what's sake anything is or is done. Certainly the Bourgeois is not an animal which exists in order to satisfy its desires (that is, exists in order to exist). But he recognizes 'neither God nor Master.' It is to express and justify this awkward state of affairs that the Bourgeois elaborates his final ideology: Utilitarianism.[28] According to this teaching man is indeed the end of all action, but neither any particular man (such as a king or Master) nor each man for himself (as with animal behavior). Instead all men are ends for all men, that is, each individual is at once both means and end. The particular is useful to the universal and vice-versa; the citizen is mediated with himself by the state, and the state with itself by each citizen.

Utilitarianism, in contrast to the previous forms of bourgeois thought, is faced by no antithetical ideology. Faith, Deism, and Idealism were all reflections of an isolated aspect of the Slave's situation, viz., his relation to the Master he recognizes above himself. Therefore they stood opposed to Pure Insight, Sensualism and

---

[28]This is how Kojève translates Hegel's *Nützlichkeit*, literally 'usefulness' or 'utility.'

Materialism which reflect the other aspect of his situation, viz., his relation to the nature beneath himself (which he transforms). But Utilitarianism reflects *service*, the link between these two aspects: the Slave transforms nature *for* his Master, that is, is useful to him, is the means to his ends. So there is no antithesis to Utilitarianism. There is, however, a duality within it: one may consider it egoistically (the particular serves the universal in order to serve himself from it) or altruistically (the particular is duty-bound to sacrifice his own interest to the universal which has graciously advanced him the means of doing so). [29]

We are close indeed to the universal mutual recognition described in the passage on the 'pure concept of recognition' in chapter IV, A. "In utility," as Hegel says, "consciousness has found its concept" (*PG*, ¶582). In other words, utilitarianism is the end and perfection of bourgeois ideology. It is not *true*, however, because it does not correspond to reality: the real world still reflects the feudal system, and thus, ultimately, the one-sided recognition of the Master by the Slave. But instead of correcting the ideology to bring it into line with France, France will be corrected to bring it into line with the ideology.[30] Truth—at least human or nonnatural truth—is *made* rather than discovered. Being does not determine consciousness; consciousness determines Being. We explained these principles above *à propos* of Hegelian anthropology, that is, Hegel's rational reconstruction of history's beginning. We shall see them further illustrated, confirmed and fulfilled in the Hegelian interpretation of the French Revolution, which marks the end of history.

M. The French Revolution

The Revolution of 1789 was not a spontaneous popular uprising against a still-vigorous despotism. Enlightenment had been sapping the strength of the *ancien régime* for a couple of generations already. So

---

[29] That there is no genuine opposition between these two interpretations Hegel has in effect already argued in chapter V, B, c: 'Virtue and the Way of the World' (see also chapter VI, B, II, a, ¶560 end). Of course, Utilitarianism may be opposed by any number of thought-forms which differ from it without being antithetical to it (see *PG*, ¶580 top).

[30] But, as with all ideologies, Utilitarianism is altered in the course of its own realization. Hegel's own post-revolutionary ethico-political teaching is, therefore, not identical with it. See again the passage from Kojève quoted above, pp 65-66.

Hegel has nothing further to add on the dissolution of the monarchy. By the time his chapter on the Revolution takes up the story, the objective universal—the state—has already disappeared: "The State only exists by the *ideas* of Particulars, by their projects for a Constitution.... *Anyone* can say 'I am the State'.... There is liberation with regard to the *given* which no longer exists, but not yet *creation* of a new *real* World. Man is in a total void: this is 'Absolute Freedom'" (*ILH*, 141-142).

We saw in chapter two what freedom is on the Hegelian view: not a thing separate from nature but a negation of natural being. It arises because man has an 'unnatural desire' for the desire of others; that is, for a kind of absence or lack. And it manifests itself in two ways, viz., the risk (potential but pure negation) of life in a struggle for the human desire of another (that is, for recognition), and the transformation (actual but impure negation) of natural being called 'work.' All freedom is thus essentially negative. But it may have a positive result: either the survival of risk (achievement of mastery) or the product of work (the artifact). The positive result depends on negation either remaining *in posse* or being 'impure'—attached to nature. Actual, pure negation is nonbeing: in human terms, death.

When the Bourgeois blunders into absolute freedom he is unaware of this. He is a romantic revolutionary who imagines, roughly, that pleasure, virtue and the law of the heart will be fully realized now that their obstacles—necessity and the way of the world—have been eliminated. In fact, these latter are obstacles only in the sense an artist's material is an 'obstacle' to the realization of his idea. Once they are eliminated there is, indeed, no more work to be done, but also no possibility of a product: no human world in which pleasure and virtue and sentiment can find a place. In Hegel's words: "Absolutely free self-consciousness finds its reality quite different from what its concept of itself was, viz., that universal will is merely the positive essence of personality.... The terror of death is the vision of [freedom's] negative essence" (*PG*, ¶ 592). Hegel thus rejects the perennially popular liberal interpretation of the 'good' French Revolution which fell into 'excesses.' Terror was implicit in the anarchy of 1789; the excesses of the Revolution *were* the Revolution.

Yet Hegel is not a counterrevolutionary of the type of Burke or De Maistre. He attributes a decisive and positive historical importance to the French Revolution: it is "heaven transplanted to earth below" (that is, the realization of the Christian ideal), and the "most sublime and last education" of man (*PG*, ¶¶ 581 and 594). We have seen plenty of freedom and negation before this. What is unique about this revolution which marks it as the culmination and end of history?

The easiest way to explain is to turn once more to the story of Master and Slave. The political embodiment of mastery is a warrior class which rules an unrecognized class of workers who see to the satisfaction of its desires.[31] And slavery is embodied by a society whose classes are leveled and merged—'in principle'—before a divine Master. Gradually this leads to the effective homogenization of the society until, on the eve of the Revolution, everyone is 'enslaved' merely to alienated human particularity, that is, wealth; the hereditary classes are a mere outward form no one any longer believes in.

The peculiar character of the French Revolution was that of being a Slave rebellion in a world without Masters, a class struggle in an implicitly homogeneous society. This distinguishes it from an ordinary dictatorship or tyranny, which depends on the existence of genuine classes, as Kojève explains:

> There is tyranny (in the morally neutral sense of the term) when a fraction of the citizens (it matters little whether it be a majority or a minority) imposes on all the other citizens its own ideas and actions that are guided by an authority which this fraction recognizes spontaneously, but which it has not succeeded in getting the others to recognize; and where this fraction imposes it on those others without "coming to terms" with them, without trying to reach some sort of "compromise" with them, and without taking account of their ideas and desires (determined by another authority, which those others recognize spontaneously). Clearly this fraction can do so only by "force" or "terror," ultimately by manipulating the others' fear of the violent death it can inflict on them. In this situation the others may be said to be "enslaved," since they in fact behave like slaves ready to do anything to save their lives (*OT*, 145).

The National Assembly, the first revolutionary government, appears as 'absolute' as any tyranny, since there is no other power to check it. But this its apparent strength is its real weakness: "It obtains power without a struggle; all which it says is law, all which it does, an act of state. But it *is not* a dictatorship precisely because nothing is *opposed* to it; it forms itself in a void. It leaves no traces in objective

---

[31]Except, of course, the desire for recognition, which it is 'unworthy' to satisfy.

reality and no one really obeys it. It cannot carry out any real, positive work" (*ILH*, 142 bottom).[32]

The second stage of the Revolution, the terror, occurs when the victorious faction of the government tries to *realize* absolute freedom. To do so it must

> effectively suppress particular wills—by death.... For there is no longer a universal will; there are only particular beings that can be reached only in their biological existence, not in their works, their actions; for they do not *do* anything (they merely "oppose" one another). Such a process can only end with the extermination of all members of the Society and the suicide of the (pseudo) dictatorship. The terror is in fact nothing but the suicide of the Society itself. (*ILH*, 143)

Elsewhere Kojève helpfully phrases the same point in the language of the Master-Slave story:

> We have seen that in the Bourgeois World there were no Masters. The Struggle [for liberation] cannot, therefore, be a class struggle properly so called, a war between Masters and Slaves. The Bourgeois is neither Slave nor Master; he is—being a Slave of capital—his *own* Slave. So it is from himself that he must free himself. And this is why the liberating risk of life takes the form not of risk on the field of battle but the risk created by Robespierre's Terror. The Bourgeois Worker, become a Revolutionary, himself creates the situation which introduces in him the element of death. (*ILH*, 194 =*IRH*, 69)

Such was the French Revolution: the first-ever homogeneous civil war. The Slave having, like the Master before him, 'revealed his essence in realizing by action his existential possibilities,' now puts an end to himself. And since Master and Slave are the two fundamental human possibilities, we may say that man himself has thereby been completed.

---

[32]In responding to Strauss in *OT* Kojève used the word 'tyranny' for what he had called 'despotism' in *ILH*.

V. THE END OF HISTORY

A.   The Last New World

Hegel's interpretation of history in chapter VI of the *Phenomenology* does not end with the French Revolution.   There follows a lengthy section devoted to Kant's moral philosophy and German romanticism.   This has understandably puzzled commentators: were Jacobi and Novalis, or even Kant, historical 'moments' comparable in importance to the Roman Empire (which is allotted less space)?

We shall not argue with those who think Hegel was exaggerating the importance of his contemporaries.   But let us see why, according to Kojève, he needed to distinguish this brief 'third historical epoch:'

> If the end of History is the *synthesis* of Mastery and Slavery, and the *comprehension* of this synthesis, these two periods [viz., of Mastery and Slavery] must be followed by a third in which human existence, somehow neutralized, synthetic, reveals itself to itself by actively realizing its own *possibilities*. And this time—these possibilities also involve that of *understanding* oneself completely and definitely, that is, perfectly (*ILH*, 173 =*IRH*, 45).

In a sense, then, history did end with the self-destruction of Christendom: there is no further 'negation of the given.'   What follows is 'merely' the establishment of a positive human reality in which all the negation—the work and struggle—of history is preserved and 'taken up.'   And, secondly, the comprehension in thought of this new and definitive reality.   Kojève interprets the third section of chapter VI as an account of various attempts to 'come to terms with' the post-revolutionary world.   These include privately condemnation of it ('conscience') and flight into a world of imagination ('the beautiful soul'). We need not linger over them.

The section and the chapter closes with an enigmatic passage on "Evil and Its Forgiveness." For Kojève, its correct interpretation provides the key to the entire work:

> As long as one does not know that the sole theme of the section is Napoleon and the criticisms of him, its content remains strictly incomprehensible.... Hegel is speaking here of himself as speaking of Napoleon. The "evil" in question is the supposed political "crime" of Napoleon, and the "forgiveness" is the justification of the Napoleonic work by Hegel's philosophy (*HMC* 361 =Eng. 38).

Kojève remarked that once he had understood the place of Napoleon in the *Phenomenology* "all Hegel was saying appeared luminous to me" (*Interview*).

Hegel's 'justification' of the conqueror was not a mere consequence of personal admiration. He could not, consistently with his own philosophical principles, have joined in condemning Napoleon regardless of his private feelings. Because, as we shall see, for the historicist to know all, he must forgive all.

B.   The Union of Real and Ideal

Hegel's 'forgiveness' of Napoleon is the unsentimental placing of an equals sign between human ideal and reality. This is the true significance of the 'end of history'—that bizarre-sounding notion with which Kojève's name will forever be associated. And, bizarre or not, the absolute necessity of such a notion within the context of historicist thought is not difficult to demonstrate. It parallels the need for a human *telos* within classical thought.

Knowledge in the strict sense (*episteme, Wissenschaft,* or scientific knowledge) is distinguished from opinion by its universality and permanence. If yesterday I thought I knew there was no such thing as a red cow, and today I come across one, I may say in retrospect that I did not genuinely have knowledge. This permanence of knowledge derives, on the classical account, from something permanent in its objects, to which the name 'nature' is given.[1] If a science of cow-color

---

[1] Some premodern teachings substitute God for nature. Plato's teaching is, as usual, a matter of interpretation: the 'forms' are spoken of as transcendent. In either case the source of permanence is *outside* the mind. (See *ILH*, 233.)

is possible, color must be part of the nature or natural essence of those animals (as opposed to a matter of chance). Analogously, if there is to be a science of human things there must, despite appearances to the contrary, be a human nature. This is understood to involve a *telos*, or natural purpose, which can be used to understand and evaluate purposive human behavior—as seen, for example, in the productive arts.

The Hegelian philosopher, no less than the Aristotelian, seeks timeless knowledge.[2] But he rejects 'human nature:' man, insofar as he is not merely an animal, *is* a product of all he has *done*. As long as he continues to act he can continue to change. Action is free, hence change is unforeseeable, hence timeless knowledge impossible. But suppose action comes to a definitive end (how and why we may consider later). Henceforward man would have an immutable essence—not a 'nature' given him from the beginning, but a nonnatural essence of his own creation. This is the true significance of the end of history. In Kojève's words: "as soon as one introduces Negativity or *crative* Action into Given-Being [sc.: in one's philosophical account], one can only claim *absolute,* or *total* and *definitive,* truth by allowing that the creative dialectical process is *finished*" (*ILH,* 533 =*IDPH,* 118 bottom).

Those who dismiss out of hand the notion of an end of history might pause to consider whether the idea that history has never begun sounds more plausible. For this is the classical teaching—that 'history' as understood by historicism does not exist, that no human action can essentially change the world, and that what is usually called 'history' is mere accident.

The argument can be put another way. Modern thought rejects any purely discursive search (in the manner of Plato's *Republic*) for an ideal standard by which to understand and judge the human world: an idea or ideal only exists insofar as it is realized by human action. If a modern doctrine is to succeed on its own terms—if it can consistently claim to be more than idle chatter or wishful thinking—its ideal must somewhere, sometime coincide with the real. Hegelianism rightly rejects the Hobbesian teaching that this happened in the beginning, at

---

Kant's rejection of this view was an important step toward Hegelian historicism.
   [2]This is all that Hegel means by the grandiose-sounding phrase 'absolute knowing'—the traditional *episteme.* *Non*-absolute knowing, a time-bound knowledge which yet is more than mere opinion, is what is original in Hegelianism.

the first formation of political society.[3] The only alternative consistent with the modern premises is for the standard to be *produced* by historical action, for an outcome rather than an origin to provide the 'realistic ideal.' Accordingly, if Hegel wished to assert that his *Phenomenology* was knowledge and not historical romance—in other words, if he was a *rational* historicist—he had to allow that the definitive human ideal had been realized at the time of his writing. The Sabbath of scientific contemplation cannot begin until the work of historical creation has been pronounced good—that is, finished or perfected.[4]

Or again, historicism may be considered from the viewpoint of moral philosophy, where it appears as a species of conventionalism:

> There is no moral philosophy of Hegel (who is hostile to moralists); only a philosophy of morality. Only axiom: the individual must live in conformity with the mores and customs of the nation [*peuple*] in which he lives (as long as the mores of the nation correspond to the *Zeitgeist*—that is, as long as they are "solid," resistant to criticism and revolutionary attacks). If not, he perishes: as a criminal or madman (*ILH*, 65).

The collective might of the state or community makes right. All ethical imperatives are hypothetical, based upon objective sanctions; moral goodness is prudence. Moreover, it is difficult to see how one could *know* the mores of one's nation to be 'solid' except by testing them. And if the Hegelian account of the French Enlightenment is any indication, it would appear that widespread 'testing of solidity' is the primary cause of *lack* of solidity. So at bottom, this view of morality gives us no practical guidance whatsoever.

Kojève believes that the conventionalist view can be saved from the slide into sheer relativism by an appeal to history. Historicism is a 'dynamic conventionalism:'

> Suppose that a man assassinates his king for political reasons. He thinks he is acting rightly. But the others treat him as a criminal, arrest him and put him to death. In these conditions, he is in fact a

---

[3]Insofar as Hobbes may have intended his account of the social compact unhistorically, as an account of the 'logical' foundations of commonwealth, he relapsed into traditional 'idealism.' Radically modern, 'realistic' thought is ineluctably historicist.

[4]Conversely, historical man's capacity essentially to change the world is related to his capacity for error, or 'freedom from truth.'

criminal.... But suppose the assassination in questions unleashes a victorious revolution. Suddenly the society treats the assassin as a hero. And in these conditions he is in fact a hero, a model of virtue and civic spirit, a human ideal. Thus man can transform a crime into virtue, a moral...error into truth (*ILH*, 465 =*IRH*, 189-190).

The objection to this is obvious: revolutions may be followed by restorations. A short-sighted historicism allows good and evil to trade places with every shift in power.

The solution is also not far to seek. If one does not wish to relapse into an appeal to transcendent, timeless standards, one must find an absolute moment in history, an epistemic equivalent of the Archimedean point:

The true moral judgments are those which the State makes (moral=legal). States themselves are judged by Universal History. But for these judgments to have a meaning History must be finished. And Napoleon and Hegel finish History. That is why Hegel can judge States and individuals. "Good" is all which prepared for Hegel, that is, the formation of the Universal Napoleonic Empire (*ILH*, 95).[5]

One might appreciate some guidance in the application of this criterion: was it, for example, Athens or Sparta, patricians or plebeians, Socrates or Christ who did more toward the coming of the Napoleonic Empire? The overall tone of Hegel's and Kojève's accounts of history is scarcely judgmental or partisan.

However that may be, Kojève certainly believed that there was a nonarbitrary morality after the end of history. This is simply identical to the laws and mores of the final political regime. Just as recommendation and description would coincide in a fully realized Hobbesian commonwealth, so "the postrevolutionary *Moralität* of the Hegelian citizen...is nothing other than a conscious grasping of *concrete reality*" (*ILH*, 94).[6]

As for the moral duty to conform to the laws of the final state—it is in the final analysis still no more than prudence. War and revolution,

---

[5]"Moral=legal" is perhaps misleading; law should probably be taken to include mores (also part of the meaning of *nomos*) which are 'enforced' by the extralegal giving and withholding of recognition, and by the 'conscience' which is sublimated or internalized recognition.

[6]Note the contrast with the *soi-disant* realism of that decadent product of later modern thought, 'value-free social science.' A world free of values is an abstraction rather than *concrete reality*; hence no science of it is truly realistic.

we are told, are no longer possible, so the would-be revolutionary (or common lawbreaker) will *in fact* always be in the wrong; the hypothetical imperative can *in fact* always be treated as if it were categorical.

C. The Universal Homogeneous State

In Chapter I we remarked, *à propos* of the theory of human nature, that proving the need for a concept within a given system of thought does nothing to demonstrate the soundness of the concept itself. The same is true in historicism. The epistemological requirement for an absolute moment in history does not show us what that moment is or how one might identify it.

Given how important the idea of an end of history is in Hegelian philosophy, it is surprising how little space Kojève devotes to describing the political reality which is said to mark it. We can quote most of the passage directly. The Napoleonic Empire, we are told, is for Hegel

> a *universal* and *homogeneous* State: it unites all of humanity (at least that which counts historically) and "subsumes" (*aufhebt*) within itself all "specific differences" (*Besonderheiten*): nations, social classes, families.... So wars and revolutions are henceforward impossible. Which is to say that this State will not change, will remain eternally identical to itself. And Man is formed by the State in which he lives and acts. So Man also will not change anymore (*ILH*, 145).

Concerning this opening section we may make three remarks. First, Kojève must begin vacillating from the very first sentence: we all know that Napoleon's Empire covered only a small portion of the earth. The solution? The rest of the world does not 'count.' Second, one wonders what could possess anyone to fix upon Napoleon Bonaparte as the historical figure whose emergence would make wars impossible.

Finally, one is puzzled by the reference to man's formation by the state. It may appear to be a lapse into the doctrine that thought is a product of material conditions (see Chapter III, note 41 above). Man before the end of history is certainly not *exhaustively* formed by the state. But after that point truth is fixed, and the Endstate, like Plato's Republic, is informed by knowledge of it. Posthistorical man is formed or educated in accordance with Hegelian science. But this is not supposed, like Platonic wisdom, to exist by nature and independently of human convention. And one of the conventions on which Hegelian science may depend is *the teaching of Hegelian science* in the State. This raises the issue of how far the Endstate is dependent upon instruction which would seem to be susceptible to alteration and even replacement.[7] It seems as if the modern doctrine that knowing is making survives the end of history somehow: the final truth about the human things requires continual maintenance by the institutions which form man. Kojève elsewhere suggests that Hegel may have hoped "to be called to Paris by Napoleon to become the Philosopher (Sage) of the Universal Homogeneous State, charged with explaining (justifying)— and perhaps directing—Napoleon's activity" (*ILH*, 154).[8] The end of history does not sound like a liberal paradise.

The passage we were citing continues:

> In the final analysis, this State does not change any more because all its Citizens are "satisfied" (*befriedigt*). I am fully and definitively "satisfied" when the personality which is exclusively *mine* is "recognized" (in its reality and worth, its "dignity") by *all*, on condition that I myself "recognize" the reality and worth of those who are supposed to have to "recognize" me. To be "satisfied" is to be "*unique* in the world and (nevertheless) *universally* valid." And this is what is realized for the Citizen of the Universal Homogeneous State. On the one hand, thanks to its universality, I am "recognized" by *all* men, who are all my *peers*. On the other hand, thanks to its homogeneity, it is really *I* who am recognized," and not my family, social class, nation (*ILH*, 145-146).

This should be compared, first of all, with the ideal Hobbesian commonwealth. We have already seen that only a universal, world state could fully embody Hobbes's recommendations. We may now add that it would have to be homogeneous in Kojève's sense: "If nature...have made man equal, that equality is to be acknowledged; or if nature have made men unequal, yet because men that think themselves equal will not enter into conditions of peace but upon equal terms, such equality must be admitted."[9] As always in Hobbes, origins are

---

[7]Historical evolution depends on memory to preserve what has been negated: see *ILH*, 503-504 =*IRH*, 232-233. What, then, would Kojève make of attempts by twentieth-century tyrannies to 'rewrite' the past?

[8]Consider, in this connection, that 'Pedagogy' becomes an increasingly important term in Kojève's later writings.

[9]*L*, xv; compare the 'eighth law of nature' in the same chapter: "that no man by deed, word, countenance, or gesture declare hatred or contempt of another."

authoritative; but what they direct is scarcely different from what Kojève's Hegelian teaching sees as established by historical action.

The paragraph we are considering should also be compared with Hegel's 'Pure Concept of Recognition:' clearly, Kojève is asserting that the Napoleonic Empire is for Hegel the historical actualization of such 'ideal' recognition. One might infer that this ideal is Hegel's criterion for deciding that history is over: knowing beforehand that only universal recognition can satisfy specifically human desire, he finds such recognition embodied in the Napoleonic state and concludes that it marks the end of history. Once again, this would be to let our Aristotelian common sense displace historicist principles.

The 'Pure Concept of Recognition,' as we said above, is written from the vantage point of the phenomenological observer. Its content was unknowable in principle to the original combatants and, indeed, to anyone before the end of history. Postrevolutionary equality is a truth created by historical action and not a 'given' aim of history. Accordingly, Hegel cannot look for satisfaction of the desire for recognition to determine whether history is finished; it is rather the whole anthropology based on the desire for recognition which is inferred after the fact from observation of the Endstate. The rational historicist reasons, in Kantian fashion, 'the end of history has such-and-such a character; what must man have been all along to rest "satisfied" with this reality?'[10]

But to continue with the passage at hand:

> The Particular (I, ego) relates directly to the Universal (State) without there being screens formed by "specific differences" (*Besonderheiten*: families, classes, nations). Which is to say that in the Postrevolutionary World Individuality is realized (for the first time) (*ILH*, 146).[11]

All natural beings are particular insofar as they are natural. In other words, in nature to be universal (that is, indeterminate in time and

---

Note how Hobbes backs away, in the second sentence quoted above, from the implication in the first that nature provides a positive standard for the disposition of the state.

[10]We have still left open the question of what criterion *is* used to establish that history is over.

[11]'Individuality' is Kojève's technical term for the synthesis of universality with particularity which, as we saw above (Chapter IV, Sections G-I), is specifically human. For a thematic discussion see *ILH*, 505-511 =*IRH*, 234-241.

space) is simply not to be. Apparent exceptions, such as the universal essences of natural kinds, are not genuinely natural: for Kojève these 'natural essences' have a reality distinct from their natural substrate only because of human discourse, which is unnatural. Humanity begins as a striving to transcend animal particularity—a striving which, in the state of nature, can only mean the risk of death. But in the human world established through such risk, a universal *being* ceases to be a contradiction in terms. The Master's status is real, not because of any *thing* in nature, but because agreed upon by Master and Slave; a convention is by definition shared by more than one person. The human world is fundamentally discursive—no less for Kojève and Hegel than for the classics, though the Hegelian sees discourse as an essential by-product of action rather than as primitive. And discourse, though essentially unlimited in time and space, is always incarnated in particular beings: spoken or written words, brain tissue, or the body in its movements (for action is simply 'meaningful behavior'). The active or purely discursive incarnating of universality in particularity is, as we said above, the human principle of individuation. The perfect active realization of individuality is the state based upon the universal principles of the French Revolution (falsely believed to be 'natural' rights of man). And, to anticipate, the perfect purely discursive realization of individuality is the mortal being in whom is incarnated the timelessly true and comprehensive discourse: the Sage, Hegel. Since history is over, Hegel's science can no longer be affected by human action, so that one could call it a 'divine *logos*;' and Hegel, in whose flesh it is incarnated, is the true Christ.

Such is the meaning of individuality at the end of history. And Kojève's description of the Endstate as an undifferentiated, unitary mass of 'individuals' undoubtedly captures something true and important about the modern Leviathan. Looking around at contemporary America, one sees religion replaced by an assortment of 'therapies,' moral duties by nebulous notions like 'self-fulfillment,' work and struggle by a narcissistic and desultory hedonism; and yet there is a very large degree of uniformity of thought, expression, and activity among the millions of 'individualists.' Many observers with no special interest in Hegel have suspected that these tendencies, far from being in conflict, have a single main source: the decay of *Besonderheiten,* of the institutions which mediate the particular with the universal. What is dubious in Kojève's thesis is that this democratic mass-state is more humanly satisfying than the possibly less just states which preceded it. And if it is not, that is perhaps because recognition, in Strauss's words, "may lose in its power to satisfy what it gains in universality" (*OT*, 210).[12]

This, however, is a minor point in comparison with what follows:

> Of course only the Head of the Universal Homogeneous State (Napoleon) is *really* "satisfied" (=recognized by all in his reality and personal worth). So he alone is truly free (more than all the Heads of State before him, who were always "limited" by "specific differences" of nation, class, family). But all the citizens are potentially "satisfied," for *each* can *become* this Head of State whose personal action is at the same time universal (*ILH*, 146).[13]

This is possibly the most anticlimactic passage in the history of philosophy. We have repeatedly stated that a potentiality only has reality for the historicist insofar as it effects something—in other words, insofar as it is actualized. But the meaning of the end of history is that man's free potentiality has been exhausted. *Potentiality-mongering* is inadmissible at this stage. Moreover, even if we could allow it we would have to extend it to earlier history: ever since the anthropogenic struggle, after all, man has been *potentially* satisfied. So the end of history does not seem to have benefited anyone but Napoleon Bonaparte. And, as Strauss points out, Hegel himself had defined 'oriental despotism' as a state in which only one man is free (*OT*, 208).

Kojève's description of the Endstate concludes as follows:

> Each can actualize his Desire for recognition: on condition of accepting (element of Mastery) the risk of death which competition involves in this State (=Political Struggle; moreover, this risk guarantees the "seriousness" of the candidates), and also on condition of having previously taken part in the constructive activity of the Society; in the collective Work which maintains the State in reality (element of Servitude, Service, which guarantees, moreover, the "competence" of the candidates).... Also, what is new in this State is that *all* are (on occasion) *warriors* (conscription) and that *all* also take part in the social *work* (*ILH*, 146).

---

[12]Strauss is merely returning to Hobbes's teaching about recognition ('honors'), according to which "man...can relish nothing but what is eminent." Perhaps the essential point was already made by Aristotle in his criticism of Plato's communism (*Politics*, II, 1262b14-19), though love is not the same as recognition.

[13]Note that Napoleon, if satisfied, can no longer negate, and thus is not free in the same sense as historical man: 'freedom' is equivocal in Kojève's usage. In *ILH*, 502 =*IRH*, 231 to be "truly free" is precisely to be "fully satisfied by what [one] is."

The abolition of the 'idle' aristocracy and imposition of the *levée en masse* is said to be the final synthesis of Mastery and Slavery. But this is not easy to 'synthesize' with the claim that "wars...are henceforward impossible." Furthermore, 'work' in the proper sense, work which negates the 'given,' is no longer possible (the so-called work of the posthistorical world being mere maintenance, as Kojève implies in this very passage).

Undoubtedly, Kojève is correct to point out that revolutionary chaos provided a harsh process of selection through work and struggle which more than compensated for the apparent liberality of opening careers to talents. The visible result was the astonishing rise of a single—undoubtedly talented—Corsican artillery captain. But it is difficult to see how such conditions could be given a self-perpetuating institutional form. The French Empire was in fact made hereditary from the moment it was proclaimed (1804). At the very time Hegel was conceiving and writing his *Phenomenology*, Napoleon was busy establishing a *noblesse d'Empire*, partly based on service to the state but also hereditary.

The underlying difficulty with the entire description of the Universal Homogeneous State is that it clearly is not made from mere passive contemplation of a final, 'given' reality. To make of the Napoleonic Empire a serviceable standard, a fixed moral and epistemic reference-point, Hegel (or Kojève) is forced to 'interpret' what he sees. The suspicion inevitably arises that the philosopher is arbitrarily reading his own speculative notions into the phenomena. This exactly parallels our suspicion voiced earlier that Hobbes had designed his supposed original compact to yield practical conclusions he preferred independently of any historical reconstruction. It is perhaps the fate of modern philosophy ever to be exposed to objections of this sort, a consequence of its determination to be 'realistic.'[14]

Hegelianism would be vulnerable to such criticism even if Napoleon had conquered Europe, or the entire world, and died on his throne. But a new set of problems arises once we try to take into account the apparent 'history' which has occurred since the

---

[14]We said, indeed, that historiographical accuracy was not an all-overriding consideration in the philosophy of history. That was because a particular historical 'work' which lives on in our own civilization might be misattributed (for example, to Greece instead of Egypt or Babylon) without the premises of historicism itself being called in question. Such a defense will not do at this stage. The ideal is supposed to be a reality before our eyes, neither a reconstruction of the past nor a prediction extrapolated from present reality and 'ideology.'

Phenomenology was written. The final state Hegel envisioned was, as Kojève admits, at most "in the process of formation" as Hegel was writing, so that he "had to anticipate the historical [?] *future*" (*ILH*, 467 =*IRH*, 192). If he was indeed doing so, it seems hardly less presumptuous a piece of armchair speculation than the apocryphal Hegel's attempt to demonstrate the impossibility of further planets being discovered; nature is, in fact, a safer bet than history!

However that may be—Kojève tells us there were

> very important modifications which Hegel had to bring to his conception following Napoleon's fall. [He thought of] substituting the Archduke of Austria for his "Napoleon" [and] finished by seeming to believe that the perfect and definitive State begun by Napoleon was realized by the Kingdom of Prussia which, however, was not "universal" and did not aspire to universality (*HMC* 363n2 =Eng. 40n6).

A strange spectacle. The philosopher runs about like a lover, straining to make out the features of his own ideal in a series of realities independent of him and outside his control—with about as much success as the average lover. Exhausted by years of pursuit of a volatile French mistress, he resigns himself to a rational marriage with a somewhat dowdy German *Hausfrau*.

Of course, various arguments are available to Hegel to justify his tacks and turns. Kojève maintains that "when writing the *Phenomenology* in 1806...he affirmed merely the presence in the World of the *germ* of [the final] State and the existence of the necessary and sufficient conditions for its spread" (*ILH*, 290 =*IRH*, 97). Afterwards, Hegel could assert that "Napoleon disappeared because he had (virtually) finished his work" (*HMC* 363n2 =Eng. 40n6).

But one is surely right to be suspicious of a philosopher's 'realistic' pretensions when everything he likes but cannot make out clearly is asserted to be realized 'in principle,' already 'essentially' decided upon and later to unfold in quasi-organic fashion (that is, without genuine work or struggle) to confound sceptics less adept than the philosopher at reading the runes of history. Similarly, anything the philosopher sees but does not like in the present might be declared the atavism of a superseded historical moment.[15] The more these sorts of

---

[15]See, for example, *ILH*, 72 bottom-73 on the "possibility of an unlimited survival of religion;" and *ILH*, 206: "The Man who rests content with the joy of pure knowledge or artistic contemplation can remain an Intellectual or Artist eternally."

arguments are used, the more arbitrary they must appear. No, better to admit that the 'ideals' which a historicist can cobble together from present or past regimes, books, or private speculation, and support with rhetorical arguments, are no less varied than the systems of 'natural right' devised by thinkers in the classical tradition. This is a serious indictment, for the original inspiration of the modern project was the desire to get past the 'airy' disputes of scholasticism by focusing on what men really do as opposed to what they should do.[16]

A final note: although Hegel's 'forgiveness' of Napoleon was, as we have said, not merely a matter of personal admiration, there is no doubt that the philosopher did esteem this consummate 'man of action' greatly, and lamented his passing. Now, it is well-known that in his later years Hegel employed grandiose, almost religious language in public and philosophical contexts when describing the political system of Prussia. There is evidence, however, that privately, he felt no such enthusiasm. Kojève speaks of his 'detesting' the Prussian State. And the reason for the discrepancy, as Kojève says, is that Hegel *had* to accept the political status quo, given that he was convinced of the final truth of his own system (*ILH*, 291 =*IRH*, 98). The end of history is analogous to Leibniz's teaching that we live in the best of all possible worlds, which ceases to appear Pollyannaish the moment one reflects on its implication that all the world's evils are necessary and irremediable (speaking *sub specie aeternitatis*). If action has definitively ceased, no ideal not already realized can provide a basis for condemning the existing human world. History appears to have gotten the last laugh on Hegel.

D.   A Hegelian World-Revolution

Man is a complaining animal; that is, he always distinguishes a way things should be from the way they are. Classical philosophy accepts this as a natural and permanent state of affairs. Plato's *Republic*, for example, emphasizes the gap between the philosophical imagination and political practice, perhaps from a belief that doing so is to the benefit of both. But modern philosophy rejects even the Aristotelian strand of classical thought as utopian. It refuses to accept

---

[16]See *OT*, 167, where Kojève writes that Hegel's "method of *historical verification* is meant "to resolve [political-philosophical questions] by going beyond *discussion* with philosophers...in order to reach 'indisputable' solutions."

any definitive separation of moral or anthropological theory and political action.

That distinction, however, lives on under another form within the modern tradition. Speaking very broadly, there is one strand of modern thought which lowers its ideal until some kind of contact with the real is assured, and another which insists upon the present or eventual receptiveness of the practical realm to the conclusions of speculation. To the former tendency we may ascribe Machiavellian *Realpolitik*, Burke's defense of prejudice and prescription, the authoritarian aspect of Hobbes and, as a kind of *reductio ad absurdum*, the 'value-free' social science bequeathed to us by positivism. The second or activist tendency appears in milder form in the practical recommendations of Hobbes, the ideal of popular enlightenment, liberal meliorism—and, for stronger tastes, as Marxism and other secular millenarian doctrines holding forth the prospect of a 'new man.'

In the present writer's view, no stable *via media* is possible between these opposed tendencies of modern thought. The career of the consummate 'modern' philosopher Alexandre Kojève perfectly illustrates the dangers of modern thought arising from this dilemma: it was a journey from radical activism to a kind of twilight resignation not far from Hegel's own.

Up to this point, we have been less concerned with either Kojève or Hegel than with 'Kojève's Hegel' an artificial persona consciously adopted by Kojève for pedagogical purposes. It bears an analogy to the characters in Plato's dialogues, who are neither simply their historical originals nor the author. But Kojève did not practice the same discretion as Plato: he let his mask slip on occasion. We must now say something of his personal views and purposes in interpreting Hegel.

Most importantly, at the time he wrote the works with which we have mainly been concerned, *Kojève did not himself believe that history was over*. For him, though not for Hegel as interpreted by him, a "*germ* of the [Universal Homogeneous] State and the existence of the necessary and sufficient conditions of its spread" (*ILH*, 290 =*IRH*, 97) are inadequate. He believed that history would not end until a classless, socialist world-state existed in reality.[17] And he emphasized that there was nothing necessary about such a development: "history

---

[17]Kojève's clearest explanation of what he understood by 'socialism' is *PD*, 575-586. He explicitly identifies homogeneity and socialism in *PD*, 571n2.

Kojève does not hold that coercive government can ever 'wither away'; some citizens of the Endstate will have to be "locked up:" *OT*, 255 (letter to Strauss).

could stop before reaching its truly insurmountable limit" (*ILH*, 404). But he did think that such a state was a necessary precondition for science or wisdom. As long as war and revolution remain possible, the essence of humanity may continue to be altered through work and struggle.

It follows that for Kojève the philosophy of Hegel cannot have been *true*. And he accepted this consequence. But, he added,

> it is not thereby necessarily an error. It would not be unless it could
> be proved that the Universal Homogeneous State [Hegel] had in mind
> was *impossible*. But this *cannot* be proved. Now, what is neither an
> error nor a truth is an idea or, if you prefer, an ideal. This idea can
> only be transformed into a *truth* by negating *action* which, by
> destroying the World which does not correspond to the idea, creates
> by that very destruction the World which conforms to the ideal. In
> other words, one can accept the anthropology of the *Phenomenology*
> while knowing that the perfect man (the Sage) with whom it is finally
> concerned has not yet been realized only on condition of wanting to
> *act* with a view to realizing the Hegelian State indispensable to the
> existence of that man—act, or at least *accept* and "justify" such an
> action if it is taken by someone somewhere (*ILH*, 290-291 =*IRH*, 97-
> 98).[18]

For Kojève, the philosopher *qua* philosopher has a stake in politics; partisanship is inseparable from 'love of wisdom.' Once again, his view represents the most extreme form of philosophical modernism.

There is a sense in which classical thought, too, might be considered partisan. In the *Republic*, for example, Socrates gives reasons for considering Spartan timocracy superior to Athenian democracy. But this 'partisanship' follows from an ideal of justice arrived at through a process of speculation essentially independent of the regime in which it occurs. Of course, philosophy requires a measure of freedom and tolerance in order to exist. But this is a dependence *per accidens*; it determines neither the direction nor the results of philosophical speculation. Thus, there was no contradiction in Socrates' assertion that a type of regime in which philosophy thrives

---

[18]Kojève allows the possibility of a provisional historicist anthropology before the end of history: "There is also a possible science of Man insofar as he belongs to the past and present. Only Man's *future* would then be given over to scepticism or faith" (*ILH*, 486 =*IRH*, 214; compare *PD*, 12-13, 327). But would not such a science be vulnerable to 'ideological' distortion? And would not the amount and direction of such distortion be rationally indeterminable?

(democracy) was inferior to one in which it could never have arisen (timocracy). And just as philosophy is not determined by the regime, so the regime may remain wholly uninfluenced by philosophy— without this constituting an objection to philosophy. The Republic described by Socrates may be the preeminently just regime even if nothing remotely like it ever exists. Furthermore, there may be a natural disharmony between wisdom and the city: even if wholly successful philosophers (that is, wise men) were to rule, they would probably have to lie to their inferiors for their inferiors' own good.

Modern thought was born in activism. Machiavelli announced the modern project with the derisive remark that

> many have imagined republics and principalities that have never been seen or known to exist in truth.... But since my intent is to write something useful to whoever understands it, it has appeared to me more fitting to go directly to the effectual truth of the thing than to the imagination of it (*The Prince*, chapter 15; sentences transposed).

Similarly, for Hobbes all the traditional systems of natural law were castles "built in the air," whereas his 'realistic' premises would allow the "truth of speculation" to be converted "into the utility of practice." Early modern philosophical activism takes the form of *enlightenment*: truth preexists and is essentially unaltered by action; it is in harmony with society; it must merely be made to inform human institutions.

But the seeds of enlightenment's destruction are found in Hobbes's own writings: the doctrines that commonwealth is radically conventional and, most especially, that knowledge involves making, that is, is a byproduct of human action. These aspects of his thought open up the possibility of a new kind of activism which sees truth as an outcome rather than a basis for action. If these ideas are worked out consistently, the result is our historicist version of Hobbism, outlined above in Chapter Two, Section K. The early version of Kojève's Hegelianism was of this kind; it emphatically belongs to the activist branch of modern thought. History not being over, there is no need to acquiesce in Hegel's own justification of the status quo. Truth has still to be established, the world is ours to create, and contemporary interpretation of Hegel can be a revolutionary call to arms.

Kojève's clearest statement of his own intentions is not found in the record of his seminar but in "Hegel, Marx and Christianity," a review essay published in 1946. The passage is so important that it must be quoted at length. Kojève begins by admitting that "the immediate appearance of a Hegelian 'left' and 'right'" constitutes a valid objection, "even from the Hegelian point of view...to Hegel's pretension of having set forth absolute truth." But, he goes on,

> if there has been a Hegelian left and right from the beginning, that is also *all* there has been since Hegel. If we abstract from survivals of the past which Hegel knew and described ("liberalism" included), and which, consequently, cannot be held up to him as a historical or "dialectical" reflection, we see that there has been strictly nothing outside of Hegelianism (conscious or otherwise), neither at the level of historical reality itself nor at that of thought and discourse which have had historical repercussions. So we cannot say...that history has refuted *Hegelianism*. We can at most assert that it has not decided between the "left" and "right" interpretations of the Hegelian philosophy. For the discussion is still going on today.
>
> Now, according to Hegel, a discussion can only be resolved by reality, that is, by the realization of one of the opposing theses. Verbal polemics or "dialectics" merely reflect the real dialectic which is a dialectic of Action manifested as Work and Struggle. And in fact it is as work ("economic system"), revolutions and wars that the polemic between Hegelians has been unfolding for nearly one-hundred-fifty years. The left has recently achieved a stunning victory, and it would be absurd to conclude that the "right" will win in the end. But it would be just as false to say that the provisionally victorious interpretation has definitively proved itself true.
>
> In our day as in the time of Marx, Hegelian philosophy is not a truth in the proper sense of the term: it is...a "project" which must realized, and thus proved, by action. What is remarkable, however, is that it is precisely because it *is* not yet true that this philosophy alone is capable of *becoming* so one day. For it is alone in saying that truth is created in time from error, and that there are no "transcendent" criteria (whereas a theistic theory is necessarily either always true or forever false). And this is why history will never refute Hegelianism, but content itself with choosing between its two opposing interpretations.
>
> It can be said that, for the moment, every interpretation of Hegel, if it is more than idle chatter, is nothing but a program of work and struggle (one of these programs being called *Marxism*). And this means that the work [*œuvre*, not *travail*] of a Hegel interpreter has the significance of a work of political propaganda (*HMC* 365-366 =Eng. 41-42).[19]

---

[19]One can hardly help observing the discrepancy between this doctrine and much of his subsequent career, in particular his reluctance to publish. Asserting the inevitability and even desirability of the vulgarization of philosophical teachings (*OT*, 173-174 top and 175 bottom: remarks on

In sum, Kojève was consciously doing what Hobbes was at most unconsciously doing: attempting through propaganda to create a new and final world in accordance with his own will. He was fond of telling people he was 'god.' In the interview we have already quoted, which was given a matter of days before his death, Kojève said:

> It's true that philosophical discourse, like history, is closed. This irritates people, this idea. That's maybe why *sages*—those who succeed to the philosophers and of whom Hegel was the first—are so · rare, not to say nonexistent. It's true that you can only adhere to wisdom if you are able to believe in your own divinity.

Kojève, like the Hegel of his interpretation, pinned his hopes on a contemporary political figure. His choice was even less fortunate than Hegel's had been: the Soviet dictator Joseph Stalin. According to Seminar participant Raymond Aron, Kojève was in the habit of declaring himself a "Stalinist of strict observance."

> That Russia painted red was governed by beasts, the language itself vulgarized, the culture degraded—he did not deny it in private. Indeed, he said it on occasion as something so obvious that only imbeciles would not know it. Those who were addressing themselves to imbeciles thought necessary to repeat it.[20]

But unfortunately (or perhaps fortunately) we do not have much information concerning Kojève's views on internal Soviet politics. What we do know is that he meant to cast Stalin in the role of realizer of his own Hegelian project—just as Hegel, by his account, had cast Napoleon. This becomes clear in his debate with Strauss, to which we now turn.

'intellectuals'), he does not seem to have relished the prospect in his particular case. Compare the letter to Strauss of 29 March 1962 in *OT*, 307-308.

[20]From Aron's memoirs; cited in Auffret, 255. Olivier Wormser, friend and colleague of Kojève's at the Ministry of Finance (and subsequently ambassador to Moscow) wrote "I do not believe for a second that he was a communist when I knew him. If he sometimes said he was or had been, it was in fun or by playing on words.... He always appeared to me quite reactionary." From "Mon ami Alexandre Kojève," *Commentaire*, no. 9, 1980, 121. Kojève sometimes described himself as a "Marxist of the right" (Auffret, 304), and called Henry Ford "the only great authentic Marxist of the twentieth century." One wonders, for all that, what sort of a career Kojève might have had in *our* federal bureaucracy.

E. Philosophy and Tyranny

Kojève held that philosophers had in fact been actors in the drama of history since classical times, even where their intent was purely speculative, even when they disdained the 'base' concerns of this world. He gave clearest expression to this view in the essay "Tyranny and Wisdom," written in response to Leo Strauss's *On Tyranny.* In that remarkable book, Strauss, starting from a close reading of Xenophon's dialogue *Hiero*, mounts an all-out attack on the whole tradition of modern thought from Machiavelli to positivism. Almost alone in his time (apart from the Thomists), he defended the intrinsic superiority and continued viability of classical thought.   In particular, he maintained the continuing practical need to keep philosophy and politics from corrupting one another.

The source of this classical doctrine is, once again, Plato's *Republic*. That dialogue begins as an inquiry into justice, which is eventually defined as a condition where each citizen limits himself to the function for which he is best suited by nature. But the description of the just regime culminates in the notion of a 'philosopher-king,' which seems impossible to reconcile with this definition of justice. The philosopher seeks general principles; the king is concerned with particulars. The philosopher investigates what is timeless; the king must keep abreast of what is happening at the moment.   The philosopher detaches himself from worldly cares; the king must be attached to the worldly good of his subjects. The philosopher-king is the most utopian proposal in the dialogue. Moreover, both halves of the concept are idealized in themselves.   The philosophers are described as routinely attaining wisdom in a period of thirty years. And as kings they are presumed able to carry out the most drastic reforms without obstacles: they deprive their subjects of wealth, homes, wives, children and religion without needing to have recourse to compulsion.

Kojève, responding to Strauss, is in agreement with the Platonic Socrates that a philosopher-king would, in principle, be at an advantage *vis-à-vis* the mere king, and this for three reasons: first, the philosopher is a master of dialectic or rational argument, and "action within an already constituted State is purely *discursive* in origin; (*OT*, 148)" second, the philosopher is (relatively) free of popular prejudices and false beliefs; third, he does not isolate or abstract particular things and situations from their concrete contexts: "he will see *farther* in space and time" (*OT*, 150).

Xenophon's *Hiero* is a dialogue concerning tyranny, which in its original signification is monarchical rule unsanctioned by law or tradition. But within the limits imposed by its subject matter *Hiero*, like the *Republic*, contains a classically utopian teaching. For, first of all, it presents an ideal. The 'wise poet' Simonides describes to the tyrant Hiero of Syracuse the best, or least bad, form of lawless rule—in Strauss's words, "the utopia of the best tyranny" (*OT*, 187). But 'ideal' and 'utopia' are not synonymous. Kojève remarks that a utopia differs from what he calls an "'active' (revolutionary) idea" in that "the utopia does not show us how, here and now, to begin to transform the given concrete reality with a view to bringing it into conformity with the proposed ideal" (*OT*, 137-138). In other words, it is the dependence of the Republic on the *coincidence* of wisdom and power, or Aristotle's characterization of the best regime as what one would *pray* for, which mark these teachings as utopian in the proper sense. And the same goes for Xenophon's teaching concerning tyranny.

> For the tyrant always has some "current business" which it is impossible to drop without first completing it. And it may well be that the nature of this business is such that to attend to it proves incompatible with the measures that would have to be taken in order to...institute the ideal state of things which [the wise man] recommends. It may also be that it takes more years to conclude "current business" than there are years in the tyrant's own life.... [For example,] Hiero draws Simonides' attention to the fact that in order to *come* to power, the tyrant necessarily has to take, let us say, "unpopular" measures.... Simonides does not deny it, but he asserts that the tyrant could *maintain* himself in power without recourse to violence, by taking appropriate measures to achieve "popularity." But Simonides does not say how to go about abrogating the "unpopular" measures without immediately imperiling the tyrant's life or power (and hence also imperiling the very reforms which he was ready to introduce...) (*OT*, 137).

Such are the difficulties, from the political side, in uniting wisdom to political action. But there are further difficulties from the philosophical side. Philosophy is a demanding pursuit which is never concluded unless and until perfect wisdom is achieved. It therefore, no less than statecraft, occupies all the time of even the most talented men who devote themselves to it. Now, if a philosopher wanted to do better than Simonides and give truly *practical* political advice, he would have to "keep up with current business on a daily basis, and hence to devote *all of [his] time* to it.... [But] to do so would mean to abandon the very quest for truth that, in his eyes, is his only authentic claim to being the tyrant's *philosophical* advisor" (*OT*, 165).

Kojève thus cogently presents, in his own name, some of the principle classical arguments for the separation of philosophy and politics.   But what would happen if, ignoring such objections, we proceeded to institute a 'philosophical' regime?   Socrates delicately hints at it by declaring that his just city can only be founded after exiling all non-philosophers over the age of ten. Kojève, in best modern fashion, is even more direct: the philosopher

> would like to lose as little time as possible in [reforming the State]. Now, if he wants to succeed *quickly*, he has to address himself to the tyrant rather than to the democratic leader. Indeed, philosophers who wanted to *act* in the political present have, at all times, been drawn to tyranny.... On the other hand, it is difficult to imagine a philosopher himself (*per impossibile*) becoming a statesman, except as some sort of "tyrant." In a hurry "to have done" with politics and to return to more noble occupations, he will scarcely be endowed with exceptional political patience.   Despising the "great mass," indifferent to its praise, he will not want patiently to play the role of a "democratic" ruler, solicitous of the opinions and desires of the "masses" (*OT*, 164-165).

For example, imagine what might have happened if Plato had secured the perfect cooperation of Dionysius of Syracuse toward the establishment of an ideal state. Kojève says that Plato would quickly have been faced with both moral conflicts and theoretical uncertainties:

> On the one hand, Dionysius, eager to carry out the "radical" reforms suggested by Plato, would surely have had to intensify the "tyrannical" character of his government more and more.   His philosophical advisor would then soon have found himself faced with "cases of conscience" as his quest for an "objective truth" embodied in the "ideal" State came into conflict with his conception of a "virtue" at odds with "violence," which he would nevertheless like to continue to practice. On the other hand, Plato, conscious (in contrast to Dionysius) of the limits of his own knowledge, would soon have become aware of having reached these limits: whereupon he would grow hesitant in his advice, and hence unable to give it *in time* (*OT*, 166).

So far, nothing in Kojève's argument is incompatible with the views of Strauss and the classics. His departure from their line of reasoning occurs when he appeals to history as providing a possible solution to the conflict:

A priori it seems plausible that history could resolve the question or conflict which the philosophers' *individual* meditations (including mine) have so far been unable to settle. Indeed, we have seen that the conflict itself...[is] due to the *finitude*...of man.... Now, history *transcends* the finite duration of man's individual existence.... If, with Hegel, one grants...that history can *reach completion*...and that [an] "absolute knowledge"...results from "understanding" or "explaining" integral history...then one can equate History...with *eternity* understood as the *totality of time...beyond* which no one single man could go, anymore than could Man as such (*OT*, 168-169).

Of course, a philosophy incorporating a doctrine of human freedom cannot rest content with an appeal to history in general; it must point to historical *facts*. Kojève goes on to provide an 'activist' interpretation of the history of philosophy. Even classical thought, while consciously rejecting political involvements, was unconsciously working toward the universality of the Endstate:

What characterizes the political action of Alexander in contrast to the political action of all of his Greek predecessors and contemporaries, is that it was guided by the idea of *empire*, that is to say of a *universal* State, at least in the sense that this State had no *a priori given* limits (geographic, ethnic, or otherwise), no *pre-established* "capital," nor even a geographically and ethnically *fixed* center destined to exercise political dominion over its periphery.... It was an utterly new political idea that only began to be actualized with the Edict of Caracalla [and] that is still not anywhere actualized in all its purity.... What might account for the fact that it was a hereditary monarch who consented to expatriate himself and who wanted to merge the victorious nobility of his native land with the newly vanquished?

One is tempted to ascribe all this to Aristotle's education and to the general influence of "Socratic-Platonic" *philosophy*.... Only the disciple of Socrates-Plato could have conceived of this unity [of the Empire] by taking as his point of departure the "idea" or the "general notion" of Man that had been elaborated by Greek philosophy. All men can become citizens of one and the same State (=Empire) because they *have*...one and the same "essence"...[, viz.,] *"Logos"* (*OT*, 170-171).[21]

---

[21]Hegel famously said that a philosophy is its time comprehended in thought, which would seem to reduce the philosopher to passively registering historical change. This is one of the few points on which Kojève explicitly distinguishes his own position from Hegel's: see *ILH*, 276-280 =*IRH*, 82-85.

The historical mission of Christian, bourgeois, 'slavish' modern thought has been to work toward homogeneity—the 'classless society.' While the influence of Socratic philosophy on Alexander is a mere historical hypothesis, here

> the filiation between philosophy and politics is...absolutely certain. The tyrant [Stalin] who here initiates the *real* political movement toward homogeneity consciously followed the teaching of the intellectual [Marx] who deliberately transformed the idea of the philosopher [Hegel] so that it might cease to be a "utopian" ideal(*OT*, 173).

The result is that "what might have appeared utopian to Xenophon has nowadays become an almost commonplace reality" (*OT*, 138).[22]

F.   From Revolution to Resignation

In the late nineteen-forties Kojève came to view the end of history not as something still to be brought about but as an accomplished fact. He never, so far as we have been able to discover, offered any explanation of what led him to change his views on this cardinal point: a strange reticence. Whatever its causes, his shift bears a resemblance to that of Hegel as Kojève himself had earlier described it: from confidence in active struggle to a resigned realism. The apparent suddenness of and lack of rational explanation for this change, we suggest, is symptomatic of an instability in modern thought itself. The refusal to allow a permanent conflict between the realms of action and contemplation has resulted not in greater harmony between them but in a logical gulf bridgeable only by blind acts of will.

In a note added to his book on Hegel fifteen years after its original publication he explained, if not the causes, at least some of the significance of his new position.

> Observing what was happening around me and reflecting on what has happened in the world since the battle of Jena, I understood that Hegel was right to see in this battle the end of history properly so-called. In and by this battle the vanguard of humanity has virtually attained its term and goal, that is, the *end* of the historical evolution

---

[22]Kojève cites (*OT*, 139) the authoritarian catholic colonial empire of Antonio Salazar as an example of the formerly utopian 'improved' tyranny possible in this happier age of Stalin—a not uncharacteristic juxtaposition.

of Man. What has happened since is merely an extension in space of the universal revolutionary potential actualized in France by Robespierre-Napoleon. From the authentically historical point of view the two world wars with their retinue of small and large revolutions have had the effect only of bringing the backward civilizations of the peripheral provinces into line with the most advanced European historical positions (real or virtual). If the Sovietization of Russia and the communization of China are anything more than or different from the democratization of Imperial Germany (through Hitlerism) or the accession of Togo to independence, or indeed the self-determination of the Papuans, it is only because the Sino-Soviet actualization of Robespierrian Bonapartism forces postnapoleonic Europe to accelerate the elimination of numerous more or less anachronistic aftereffects of its prerevolutionary past (*ILH*, 436 =*IRH*, 160).

We meet the same style of argument noted before: a certain ideal is said to have been "virtually attained," yet partially obscured by "anachronistic aftereffects." It is true that all real and any possible future political developments can be accounted for in this way, but the theory correspondingly lacks specificity—it is unfalsifiable. For example, although Kojève was unwavering in his opposition to Hitler and active in the French resistance, he is right to imply in this passage that National Socialism can be understood within the context of Hegelian historicism as a means of democratization. How, indeed, could one who had cast Stalin as the homogenizer of the universal state find Hitlerian *Gleichschaltung* anything but 'progressive?'

We may also note that claiming to have discovered a 'virtual' state of affairs within the messier real one sounds suspiciously similar to discovering a 'true good' underlying all the apparent goods actually pursued.

In his early, activist period, Kojève spoke of the future end of history in wholly positive terms, as a time when man would become truly free and perfectly actualize his specifically human potentiality. Strauss, however, in his response to "Tyranny and Wisdom," had already posed some objections to this view of the matter:

This end of History would be most exhilarating but for the fact that, according to Kojève, it is the participation in bloody political struggles as well as in real work...which raises man above the brutes.... The state through which man is said to become reasonably satisfied is, then, the state in which...man loses his humanity. It is the state of Nietzsche's "last man" (*OT*, 208).

In a letter to Strauss written just after receiving this essay, Kojève in effect admitted the validity of this reasoning:

..."not human" can mean "animal" (or better—automaton) as well as "God." In the final state there naturally are no more "human beings" in our sense of a *historical* human being. The "healthy" automata are "satisfied" (sports, art, eroticism, etc.), and the "sick" ones get locked up. As for those who are not satisfied with their "purposeless activity" (art, etc.), they are the philosophers (who can attain wisdom if they "contemplate" enough.) By doing so they become "gods." The tyrant becomes an administrator, a cog in the "machine" fashioned by automata for automata.

All this seems to me rather "classical." With the one difference that according to Hegel all this *is* not right from the start, but only *becomes* right at the end (*OT*, 255).[23]

Indeed, after the end of history man becomes essentially a *zoon logon echon*: "Man does not become an animal since he continues to *speak* (negation takes place in the dialectical *thought* of the Sage)" (*ILH*, 492n =*IRH*, 220n19).

But what if rational thought, originally a by-product of active negation, cannot survive the completion of such negation? In the second edition of his Hegel book Kojève writes:

"*The definitive annihilation* of Man *properly so called*" also means the definitive disappearance of Human Discourse (*Logos*) in the proper sense. Animals of the species *Homo sapiens* would react to sonorous or mimed signals by conditioned reflexes, and their so-called "discourse" would thus be similar to the supposed "language" of bees. What would disappear, then, is not only Philosophy or the search for discursive Wisdom, but also that Wisdom itself (*ILH*, 436 =*IRH*, 160).

The posthistorical world, as conceived by Kojève at this point, is in effect like the world as explained, not by classical philosophy, but by naturalistic anthropology.

---

[23]Strauss, in *Thoughts on Machiavelli*, 298, wrote: "The domination of necessity remains the indispensable condition of every great achievement and in particular [Machiavelli's] own: the transition from the realm of necessity into the realm of freedom will be inglorious death of the very possibility of human excellence." Kojève underlined this sentence in his copy and in the margin wrote "cf Kojève." See Michael Roth, "Natural Right and the End of History: Leo Strauss and Alexandre Kojève," 417.

The vanguard of the new subhumanity is not Soviet Russia but that secure and commodious commonwealth, the United States of America:

> From a certain point of view the United States has already reached the final stage of Marxist "communism," seeing that, practically, all the members of a "classless society" can already appropriate everything they like without, for all that, having to work more than they care to.
>
> Now, several comparative voyages made (between 1948 and 1958) to the United States and the U.S.S.R. gave me the impression that if Americans have the appearance of Sino-Soviets become wealthy, it is because the Russians and Chinese are merely Americans who are still poor—on the path, moreover, to rapid enrichment. I was led to conclude from this that the American way of life was the sort of life proper to the posthistoric period, the actual presence of the United States in the World prefiguring the future "eternal present" of humanity as a whole. Man's return to animality, therefore, appeared to be no longer as a possibility yet to come but as a certainty already present (*ILH*, 436-437 =*IRH*, 161).

Quite apart from the question of how accurate his view of the United States was, we find this extreme version of the abolition of humanity implausible, even from Kojève's point of view. Discourse should cease in the sense that no *new* discourse is created, just as painting ceases when an artist puts down his brush—but that is not identical to the destruction of his finished painting. On the classical view discourse never was a human creation. We find the interpretation suggested in the letter to Strauss more compelling, according to which the posthistorical world resembles the world thought to be 'natural' in classical philosophy. Even if the posthistorical *nomoi* cannot be essentially and positively changed, yet something like history would have to begin again with the birth of each child. The shift in emphasis from 'work and struggle' to 'pedagogy' in Kojève's later writings indicates an increasingly classical view of the function (but not the origin) of philosophy.

Kojève eventually came to a slightly more hopeful view of the end of history, in which human negativity, though no longer a force for political change, might be preserved in a kind of aestheticism. The impetus for this third and final version of the end of history came not from philosophical reading or reflection, but, he tells us, from a visit to Japan in 1959:

Pure *Snobbery* there creates disciplines negative of the "natural" or "animal" given which far surpass in efficacy those which arose, in Japan or elsewhere, from "historical" Action, that is, from military and revolutionary Struggles or forced Work. Of course, the peaks (nowhere equaled) of specifically Japanese snobbery which are Noh theater, the tea ceremony and the art of flower arrangement were and remain the exclusive prerogative of the noble and wealthy. But, despite persistent economic and social inequalities, all Japanese without exception are currently capable of living according to totally *formalized* values, that is, values completely void of "human" content in the sense of "historic" content. Thus, at the limit, every Japanese is in principle capable of proceeding, out of pure snobbery, to a perfectly "gratuitous" suicide (the classical samurai's sword being replaceable by an airplane or torpedo), which has nothing to do with the *risk* of life in a Struggle carried on according to "historical" values of social or political content. Which seems to allow one to think that the interaction recently began between Japan and the Western World will finally result not in a rebarbarization of the Japanese but in a "Japanization" of Westerners (including the Russians) (*ILH*, 437 =*IRH*, 161-162).[24]

Undoubtedly this is a less grim view of the end of history. But, one wonders, why would the posthistorical world first take the shape in Japan? Because, as Kojève tells us, Japanese society

is alone in have made a nearly three-century experiment of life in the period of the "end of History," that is, in the absence of any civil or external war (following the liquidation of "feudalism" by the commoner Hideyoshi and the artificial isolation of the country conceived and realized by his noble successor Yiyeasu) (*ILH*, 437 =*IRH*, 161).

A civilization hardly influenced by Greece or by Christianity made an "experiment" in the end of history (that is, in homogeneity, and with isolation providing an ersatz universality) two-hundred years before Napoleon and Hegel! Taken literally, this remark liquidates the rest of Kojève's teaching. For it implies that the distinguishing features of the Endstate are attainable or replicable apart from the unique series of free acts of work and struggle which make up European history. But this, of course, is just the traditional doctrine of natural right: that man's end is in principal equally attainable (or unattainable) everywhere and at all

---

[24]On the relation of suicide to struggle see *ILH*, 517-518 notes =*IRH*, 248 notes.

times.   Perhaps Kojève's remarks are partly ironic.   But then it is difficult to say just what the example of Japan does show us.

In sum, Kojève's personal evolution, as well as the ambiguous character of each successive view of the end of history he held, suggest that rational historicism is every bit as flexible a teaching as traditional natural right.   And since Kojève's rational historicism is the most radical and consistent form of modern thought, it may be said that modernism's attempt to resolve traditional philosophical disputes through moral and political 'realism' has not succeeded.

G.   Conclusion: the Idea of Historicist Wisdom

We have still left unanswered what may be the most important question of all for a rational historicist, viz., what is the criterion for determining that history is over?   Kojève admits that empirical evidence by itself can never be conclusive.   Speaking once again in the persona of Hegel, he says:

> How can we know that the stabilizing of the historical "movement" in the [Napoleonic] Empire is not a mere pause, the result of a passing lassitude?   What entitles us to assert that this State will not engender in Man a new Desire other than that for Recognition, and that it will not consequently be negated someday by a negative or creative Action (*Tat*) other than Work and Struggle?
>
> We can only assert this by supposing that the Desire for recognition exhausts *all* human *possibilities*. But we are only entitled to make this supposition if we have a complete and perfect—that is, universally and definitively ("necessarily") valid, that is, *absolutely true*—knowledge of Man.   Now, by definition [for the historicist], absolute truth can only be attained at the end of History.   But it is precisely that end of History which was to be determined.
>
> We are thus involved in a *vicious circle* (*ILH*, 468 =*IRH*, 192-193).

Kojève responds that wisdom itself—that is, complete and perfect knowledge—is the criterion which establishes that history is over; and that the criterion distinguishing wisdom from philosophy and other forms of discourse is itself discursive.   In other words, while Hegelian science by its own account cannot emerge until the work and struggle of history are over, it carries the guarantee of its veracity within itself: it is not logically dependent upon the historical contingencies which led up to it.

This is hardly a surprising doctrine, or one difficult to understand. It is analogous to the case of a proposed solution to a difficult mathematical problem. One does not, in attempting to evaluate the solution, inquire into whether the mathematician in working on it was drunk or sober, whether his previous mathematical training was adequate to his attempting it, etc. The criteria for evaluating a mathematical solution are themselves mathematical. But that is not to deny that the arrival of *this particular* mathematician at the answer was contingent upon the absence of certain brain lesions, his being awake and alert, and a host of other nonmathematical circumstances.

But this analogy (which is no more than an analogy) should not lead us to trivialize Kojève's understanding of wisdom. It stands in stark contrast, for example, to the classical view.

Plato, who probably did not believe in the possibility of actualizing wisdom, bequeathed to the philosophical tradition an unforgettable image of it: the ascent from a cave. Full knowledge is to ordinary opinion as natural objects are to shadows. Philosophy is a breaking free of the artificial constraints of convention and an approach to a higher and preexistent natural world.

This image has been accepted by readers in the most different historical situations as capturing what they actually experience in the course of philosophical study. But in one way it is undoubtedly an oversimplification. Philosophizing is a gradual, and on the Platonic view never completed, process. There does not seem to be any unambiguous test for determining that one has entirely left the cave. The philosopher in this tradition is forced, in Kojève's words, to the position that

> the necessary and sufficient criterion of truth consists in the feeling of "evidence" that is presumably prompted by the "intellectual intuition" of the real and of Being, or that accompanies "clear and distinct ideas" or even "axioms," or that immediately attaches to divine revelations. This criterion of "evidence" was accepted by all "rationalist" philosophers from Plato to Husserl, passing by way of Descartes. Unfortunately, the criterion itself is not at all "evident," and I think that it is invalidated by the sole fact that there have always been *illuminati* and "false prophets" on earth, who never had the least doubt concerning the truth of their "intuitions" or of the authenticity of the "revelations" they received in one form or another (*OT*, 153).

Philosophers in the classical tradition hold that man is a part of nature, and as a corollary, that there is a natural harmony between the human mind and the world: our ideas correspond (when all goes well) to the natural essences of things. But, as Kojève suggests in this passage, there is always a certain leap of faith involved in the traditional view. However strong our certainty, or however cautious and painstaking the process by which we arrive at it, we cannot, like gods positioned outside the cosmos, test the adequation of mind or discourse to nature. So we may say that on the classical teaching there is no immanent or discursive criterion for wisdom.

Hobbes rejected the notion of a natural harmony between the human mind and the natural world. Consequently, although he aspired to a strict materialism, he was forced to admit that all knowledge of nature was irreducibly hypothetical. What man can know in the strict sense and without qualification is the world of his own creation: the world of art and convention. In Hobbesian epistemology, in other words, collective self-consciousness has primacy over consciousness.[25]

Hegel himself may have been less 'modern' than Hobbes on this point, having included a philosophy of nature in his system; his doctrine concerning natural knowledge is at best ambiguous and at worst inconsistent. Kojève's discussion of Hegel for once takes on a sharp edge: he speaks of Hegel's "absurd philosophy of Nature, his crazy [insensée] critique of Newton, and his own 'magical' physics which discredited his system" (ILH, 378 =IRH, 146).[26] Kojève's own Hegelianism, however, is once again intransigently modern. Like Hobbes, he understands humanity as distinct from rather than as a part of nature. This leads him to the initially implausible-sounding view that nature is merely an abstraction. 'To abstract,' as Kojève points out, means 'to take out of.' And in the final analysis there is only one thing not taken out of anything else: the universe, in its full spatial *and temporal* extent. This, of course, includes the human race. Nature, the nonhuman world, is therefore as much an abstraction as is 'pure humanity.'[27] Hence there is no strictly 'objective' account of nature: "The scientific experiment disturbs the Object by the active intervention of the Subject who applies to the Object a *method* of investigation belonging to himself and to which nothing corresponds in

---

[25]A fuller treatment of the history of modern thought than we can allow ourselves here would allot much space to the Kantian doctrine that nature is constituted (*qua* nature) by the mind, that is, that natural knowledge is itself at bottom a form of self-consciousness.

[26]Kojève says that it was the classical tradition which led Hegel into error on this point: see *ILH*, 485n =*IRH*, 213.

[27]Since the human subject is as much an abstraction as the natural object, this doctrine should not be considered a form of idealism. Kojève denies that Hegel was an idealist in the accepted sense of the word (*ILH*, 427-434 =*IRH*, 150-151), and makes equally clear that he himself is not (*CTD*, 177-183).

the Object itself (*ILH*, 454).[28] Kojève, who was a careful student of quantum mechanics, points out that Heisenberg's uncertainty principle is a vindication from within the natural sciences of this philosophical point.

Quantum mechanics also introduced the principle of 'complementary notions,' according to which physical reality may be spoken of either as corpuscular or as a wave filling all of space. These models are contradictory rather than complementary when we *speak* of them; but no such contradiction occurs in the mathematics, and the predictive power of the theory is unimpaired. More grist to the Hobbesian-modernist mill says, in effect, Kojève:

> This *abstract* description [of the natural world by quantum mechanics] is made not by words having a meaning (*Logos*), but with the help of algorithms: if the concrete Man *speaks* of the Real, the abstract Subject of physics uses a mathematical "language." At the level of the algorithm there is neither uncertainty nor contradiction. But neither is there *Truth* in the proper sense, since there is no genuine *Discourse* (*Logos*) revealing the Real. And as soon as one wishes to go from the algorithm to *physical* Discourse, one introduces contradictions and an element of uncertainty. So there is no Truth in the domain of Physics (and of science in general). Only philosophical Discourse can arrive there, for it is alone in relating to a *concrete* Real, that is, to the *totality* of the reality of Being (*ILH*, 455 =*IRH*, 178).[29]

In short, human discourse can, in the final analysis, only refer to a *humanized* world. Nature cannot merely be spoken of only in a hypothetical and imperfect way; rather, it cannot be *spoken* of at all.

If we wished to write a Kojèvian equivalent of the parable of the cave, we should have to imagine the philosopher not as ascending from cave to sunlight but rather as proceeding to a second cave. He is able to gain a certain perspective on the first one by comparing its shadows with the new ones before his eyes. Soon he discovers that there is a new passageway from the second cave, which leads him to a third.

---

[28]This is also the gist of Hegel's critique of what he calls *Reflexionsphilosophie*, "which reflects *on* the Real while situating itself *outside* it, without one's being able to say exactly where; a Reflection which pretends to give an 'overview' of the Real from the viewpoint of a knowing Subject which styles itself autonomous or independent of the Object of knowledge; a Subject which, according to Hegel, is only an artificially isolated aspect of the known or revealed Real" (*ILH*, 450 =*IRH*, 172-173).

[29]Is not the transition from quantum mechanics to natural science "in general" rather hasty?

Finally, after much labor, his journey takes him in a circle back to the cave from which he originally set out. At this point, having seen all the caves and verified that there is no passage out of all caves as such—no way up to sunlit nature—he may be said to possess a kind of 'absolute knowledge' of his world. From the Platonic point of view, Kojève's Hegelianism amounts to a kind of 'speleology of the spirit.' The sage, or wise man, who achieves perfect knowledge is defined by Kojève as

> the man capable of answering in a *comprehensible* or satisfying way *all* questions that may be put to him as to his acts, and answering in such a way that the *entirety* of his answers form a *coherent* discourse. Or, what comes to the same thing: the Sage is the man who is *fully* and *perfectly self-conscious* (*ILH*, 271 =*IRH*, 75-76).

At first blush the sage sounds like a disappointingly introverted or navel-gazing sort. But one must recall that for the Hegelian a 'self' is an abstraction. Since we are indissolubly linked to the whole of the historical and natural world, *perfect* self-consciousness requires full consciousness of all the essential traits of the world around us:

> One can pose any question about any of our acts—e.g, that of washing, or paying taxes—to arrive, after a few responses eliciting each time a new 'why,' at the problems of the relation of soul and body, of individual and State, at questions regarding the finite and the infinite, death and immortality, God and the World, and finally at the problem of *knowledge* itself, of the coherent and significant language which allows us to ask and answer questions....
>   In sum, to be able to answer *all* questions regarding *any* of our acts is in the final analysis to be able to respond to all possible questions *in general*.... To be perfectly and fully *self*-conscious is to have—at least virtually—an *encyclopedic* knowledge in the strong sense of the word (*ILH*, 271-272 =*IRH*, 76).

Even assuming that one can acquire such knowledge, however, one is left with the question of how to know that it *is* indeed complete an definitive. For, as Aristotle said, demonstration must begin somewhere. And it would seem that the beginning would have to be undemonstrated and perhaps nondiscursive (an 'experience' of some sort, or perhaps a divine revelation). But Hegel, according to Kojève, found a way out of this ancient difficulty:

> Hegel is, I believe, the first to have found *an* answer (I do not say *the* answer) to the question of how to know whether the knowledge one has of *oneself*, and consequently one's knowledge *in*

general, is or is not *total, unsurpassable, immodifiable,* that is, *universally* and *definitively* valid or *absolutely* true. This answer is given, according to him, by the circularity of knowledge. The Sage's "Absolute Knowledge" is *circular,* and *all* circular knowledge (there is, moreover, only one possible) is the "Absolute Knowledge" of the Sage.

In posing any question one arrives sooner or later, after a more or less long series of questions-and-answers, at one of the questions inside the circular knowledge the Sage possesses. Starting from this question and progressing logically, one *necessarily* arrives at the starting-point. Thus, one sees that one has exhausted *all* possible questions-and-answers. In other words, one has gotten a *total* response: each part of Circular Knowledge has for its answer the *whole* of this Knowledge (*ILH,* 287-288 =*IRH,* 94).[30]

In sum, wisdom is the criterion for the end of history, and circularity is the criterion for wisdom. So if the closure (as well as consistency and 'essential' completeness) of Hegelian discourse can be demonstrated, we would, indeed, have to accept the end of history—interpreting subsequent events as 'inessential,' and so on.

Kojève was not satisfied that Hegel's own system was truly circular (*ILH,* 291n =*IRH,* 98n). In any case, his rejection of the philosophy of nature would require a radical revision of the system as outlined by Hegel. It was his ambition for many years to produce such an 'updating' [*mise à jour*] of Hegelian science. Judging by what little he left in the way of hints and outlines, it would have looked very different from Hegel's *Encyclopedia of the Philosophical Sciences.*[31] But Kojève seemed to prefer settling down at the threshold of the temple: his later years were spent (when not negotiating trade agreements or founding the E.E.C.) writing eighteen-hundred pages of introductory material for a system he never seriously began.[32] In the end, the project appears to have been given up. Kojève leaves us only

---

[30]Kojève never explains why only one circular system is possible, nor what sort of 'necessity' links the steps: it cannot be logical or deductive necessity in the ordinary sense.

[31]See Kojève's *Kant,* Paris: Gallimard, 1973, 172, for a most exiguous outline of the intended system. Bernard Hesbois does his best to flesh it out from unpublished notes and occasional asides in Kojève's later writings: see "Le Livre et la mort: essai sur Kojève," unpublished dissertation, Université Catholique de Louvain (Belgium), 1985. There is a summary in Auffret, 385-402.

[32]These now fill five volumes: *CTD,* the three volumes of *EHRPP,* and *Kant.* One would gladly forgo the one-hundred-seventy pages of which Proclus is deemed worthy for an equally substantial outline or fragment of Kojève's own system.

with an 'idea' of, or project for, historicist wisdom—not the thing itself. Perhaps the conviction that it was no longer possible in the posthistorical world to say anything essentially new had something to do with his lack of urgency.

We will give Kojève word. In an interview, a few days before his death, he said:

> It's true that philosophical discourse, like history, is closed. This irritates people, this idea. That's perhaps why sages – those who succeed to the philosophers and of whom Hegel was the first – are so rare, not to say nonexistent.
>
> It's true you can only adhere to wisdom if you are able to believe in your own divinity.

EPILOGUE

The foregoing study was written in 1993-96. I have updated the references and made some stylistic changes. I would like to add a few words concerning how it came to be written, and concerning the course of history since Kojève announced its end.

I was introduced to Hegel's *Phenomenology of Spirit* as a young student, and Kojève was brought to my attention merely as a possible aid to the comprehension of that mysterious and difficult book. I happened upon a five-dollar copy of *Introduction à la lecture de Hegel* in a used bookshop; it lay unopened on my shelf for many months. During a period of leisure following the end of my formal studies, I carried out a long-cherished ambition of reading the entire *Phenomenology* in German, using Kojève's French interpretive work for elucidation.

Strauss was originally a separate interest. I studied *Natural Right and History* alongside Hegel and Kojève, and it provided the understanding of the history of philosophy which underlies the present work. My initial idea was to study the evolution of the concept "nature" from Plato to Hegel. Early on, however, I came to agree with Strauss in seeing Hobbes as a pivotal figure in the development from antiquity to Hegel, and restricted my attention accordingly.

Indeed, much of this study seems to me overly prone to identify modern thought exclusively with thinkers Strauss considered important: Machiavelli, Hobbes, Locke, Rousseau, Kant, Hegel, Nietzsche. But that does not seem to me a sufficient reason for attempting to overhaul my work eight years after completing it. There is even a certain pedagogical advantage to keeping the historical purview artificially narrow.

It seems to me appropriate, in assessing Kojève's legacy, to consider what has developed from the European Economic Community he helped to found, namely, the European Union. This former "free trade zone" turned political Behemoth has unquestionably developed an official self-understanding of Kojèvian overtones.

The new masters of Europe recently issued a draft constitution full of pompous verbiage about 'social progress, peace, justice and solidarity throughout the world' and the 'fundamental values of humanism and equality.' They inform their subjects that the European Union shall continue to march along the 'path of civilization, progress and prosperity, for the good of all its inhabitants, including the weakest and most deprived.'

At the same time these admirable humanitarians have been moving to criminalize opposition to their project. In November 2001, the European Commission adopted a "framework decision on combating racism and xenophobia," these being defined as "belief in race, color, descent, religion or belief, national or ethnic origin as a factor determining aversion to individuals." It is easy to see that what is being outlawed here is simply what remains in the way of realizing the Universal Homogeneous State: namely, the attachment of ordinary human beings to historically determined particulars of nation, kin and creed community.

Japan has avoided many of the troubles besetting Europe. But this has not been, as Kojève would have it, because of a three hundred year experiment with the End of History. It is because the Japanese have clung stubbornly to their own particularity. They have never permitted immigration. They cherish an intense national self-consciousness often expressed in explicitly racial terms shocking to "progressive" Westerners. Perhaps Japan's destiny is to become, not the trailblazer of post-humanity, but the last nation on earth where historical humanity survives.

One of the oddest developments of recent years, to my mind, has been the rise to power in America of the "Straussians" – self-proclaimed disciples of Kojève's philosophical adversary – who are in fact aggressive proponents of the Universal Homogeneous State. These men wish to impose an egalitarian regime upon the entire world, and view American military power as the most convenient means to realizing their designs. It has even been alleged in the popular press that Strauss is somehow the secret mastermind behind the second Bush administration's drive for foreign conquest.

Review of A. Delp, "Tragische Existenz." *Recherches philosophiques* 5 (1935-1936), 415-419.
>Unfortunately only an abridgment of the review as written by Kojève. Some of the suppressed material is reproduced in Auffret, 381-385. Together they give Kojève's settling of accounts with Heidegger.

"Christianisme et communisme." *Critique* 3-4 (1946), 308-312.
>Review of an anticommunist polemic by his friend and former Hegel-seminar participant Gaston Fessard, S. J.

Review of G.R.G. Mure, "A Study of Hegel's *Logic*." *Critique* 54 (1951), 1003-1007.
>Draws distinction between 'commentary' and 'interpretation', thereby shedding light on Kojève's intentions in his *interpretation* of Hegel.

"Les romans de la sagesse." *Critique* 60 (1952), 387-397.
>Playful review of three novels by Raymond Queneau, seminar participant and editor of *ILH*: the not particularly learned heros are cited as examples of posthistorical 'sages.'

"Le dernier monde nouveau." *Critique* 111-112 (1956), 702-708.
>Review in the same veine of two novels by Françoise Sagan.

"L'empereur Julien et son art d'écrire." Published in English translation in *Ancients and Moderns: Essays on the Tradition of Political Philosophy in Honor of Leo Strauss*, ed. J. Cropsey. New York, 1964.
>Written 1958; applies Strauss's interpretive principles ('esoteric writing') to the works of Julian the Apostate.

"L'origine chrétrienne de la science moderne." *Mélanges Alexandre Koyré*, vol. 2. Paris, 1964.

"Les peintures concrètes de Kandinsky." *Revue de métaphysique et de morale*, vol. 90, no. 2 (1985), 149-171.

C.   Other works referred to or consulted

Aristotle. *The Complete Works of Aristotle: The Revised Oxford Translation*. Edited by Jonathan Barnes. Princeton: Princeton University Press, 1984.

_____. *Aristotle's Nicomachean Ethics*. Translated by Hippocrates G. Apostle. Grinnell, Iowa: The Peripatetic Press, 1984.

_____. *The Politics*. Translated by Carnes Lord. Chicago: University of Chicago Press, 1984.

Auffret, Dominique. *Alexandre Kojève: La Philosophie l'État, la fin de l'Histoire*. Paris: Éditions Grasset & Fasquelle, 1990.

Burke, Edmund. *Reflections on the Revolution in France.* Edited, with introduction and notes, by J. G. A. Pocock. Indianapolis: Hackett Publishing Company, 1987.

Fukuyama, Francis. *The End of History and the Last Man.* New York: Macmillan, Inc., The Free Press, 1992.

Guthrie, W. C. K. *A History of Greek Philosophy,* vol. 3. Oxford: Oxford University Press, 1969.

Hegel, G. W. F. *Phänomenologie des Geistes.* Edited by Hans-Friedrich Wessels and Heinrich Clairmont. Hamburg: Felix Meiner Verlag, 1988.

_____. *Hegel's Phenomenology of Spirit.* Translated by Arnold V. Miller with a foreword by J. N. Findlay. Oxford: Oxford University Press, 1977.

Hesbois, Bernard. "Le Livre et la mort: essai sur Kojève." Unpublished philosophy dissertation. Université catholique de Louvain (Belgium), 1985.

Hobbes, Thomas. *The English Works of Thomas Hobbes of Malmesbury.* 11 volumes. Edited by Sir William Molesworth. London: John Bohn, 1839.

_____. *Leviathan.* Edited by C.B. Macpherson. New York: Penguin. Books USA Inc., 1968.

_____. *Man and Citizen.* Edited with an Introduction by Bernard Gert. Indianapolis: Hackett Publishing Company, 1991.
Partial translation of *De Homine* and complete translation of *De Cive.*

Machiavelli, Niccolò. *The Prince.* Translated by Harvey Mansfield. Chicago and London: University of Chicago Press, 1985.

Plato. *The Republic of Plato.* Edited and translated by Allan Bloom. Second edition, n.p.: Harper Collins, Basic Books, 1991.

Queneau, Raymond. "Premières confrontations avec Hegel." *Critique,* nos. 195-196 (August-September), 694-700.
Memoir of Kojève by comic novelist who was also a participant in his Hegel seminar, editor of *ILH,* and subject of Kojève's review essay "Les romans de la sagesse."

Rosen, Stanley. *Hermeneutics as Politics.* Oxford: Oxford University Press, 1987.
Chapter Three, also called "Hermeneutics as Politics," devoted to Kojève-Strauss debate.

Roth, Michael S. *Knowing and History: Appropriations of Hegel in Twentieth-Century France.* Ithaca: Cornell University Press, 1988.
Three chapters on Kojève.

_____. "Natural Right and the End of History: Leo Strauss and Alexandre Kojève." *Revue de Métaphysique et de Morale*, no. 3, 1991, 407-422.

Rousseau, Jean-Jacques. *Oeuvres Completes.* Edited by Bernard Gagnebin and Marcel Raymond. Paris: Gallimard, 1964.

Strauss, Leo. *The Political Philosophy of Hobbes: Its Basis and Its Genesis.* Translated by Elsa M. Sinclair: Oxford: The Clarendon Press, 1936.

_____. *Natural Right and History.* Chicago: University of Chicago Press, 1953.

_____. *On Tyranny.* Third revised and expanded edition, including Kojève's "Tyranny and Wisdom," "Strauss's "Restatement on Xenophon's *Hiero*," and the Strauss-Kojève correspondence. Edited by Victor Gourevitch and Michael S. Roth. New York, 1991.

_____. *Thoughts on Machiavelli.* Chicago: University of Chicago Press, 1958.

_____. *Hobbes' Politische Wissenschaft und Zugehrige Schriften.* Edited by Heinrich und Wiebke Meier. Stuttgart: Metzler Verlag. 2001.

_____. "On the Basis of Hobbes's Political Philosophy." In *What Is Political Philosophy?* Glencoe, Illinois: The Free Press, 1959.

Wormser, Olivier. "Mon ami Alexandre Kojève." *Commentaire*, no. 9 (Spring 1980), 120-121.